THE SKI BOOK

D0544131

II. Ski-Rennen in GLARUS 23/24. Januar 1904.

In days of old when nights were cold, and bindings weren't invented ... At the turn of the century skiing was already a major sport, although things were a little different. Skiers like the one in this shot simply had their feet strapped to their skis. In the event of a nasty fall either the straps broke or their legs did. It was a great incentive not to fall. The single pole was used rather interestingly. For some turns the skier would put it between his legs like a witch's broomstick and, digging the tip into the snow, use it to steer himself.

THE SKI BOOK

ARTHUR SANDLES

ELM TREE BOOKS
HAMISH HAMILTON LONDON

First published in Great Britain, 1975
by Elm Tree Books Limited
90 Great Russell Street London WC1

Copyright © 1975, Arthur Sandles

SBN 241 89202 3

Cover design by Norman Reynolds
Cover photograph by Peter Runyon, Vail Associates, Colorado
Line drawings by Gill Leach

The publishers would like to thank both Corinne McCarthy and the Swiss National Tourist Office for permission to reproduce their photographs.

Produced in association with Thomson Holidays

Filmset and printed in Great Britain by
BAS Printers Limited, Wallop, Hampshire
Bound by Ebenezer Baylis, Worcester

Contents

APPENDICES

List of Illustrations

The author

Arthur Sandles is leisure editor of the *Financial Times*, and a specialist writer on travel, entertainment and sport. He learned to ski as most Britons do—in an Austrian village while on a package tour. Since then he has skied extensively in Europe and North America and written and broadcast on the subject. He is deputy chairman of the Guild of Travel Writers, was born in Durham and now lives in the City of London. He has three daughters.

Author's notes

The preparation of a book such as this involves a great deal of assistance from friends and people who become friends. My thanks go to the numerous resort officials who have given their time, ski instructors who have given their patience, and hoteliers who have somehow produced meals at odd hours for an itinerant skier.

I am particularly grateful to Thomson Holidays for their co-operation, to British Airways who appear to have routes to all the right ski places, to United Airlines, whose services seem to be designed solely for skiers, and to Air Canada. It would be churlish not to thank the Avis personnel at Munich and Geneva for their helpfulness, too.

Among the tourist officers considerable help came from Norbert Burda, Austria's man in London, Pauline Hallam (France), Knut Svorr (Norway), and Stephen Danos (Spain). Assistance way beyond the call of duty came from the Ski the Rockies organisation and from the tourist authority in Alberta (Canada). Personal thanks to Erna Low, Mark Heller, Brian Jackman, Michael Evans of Pindisports, and to Ernst and Erika Spiess in Mayrhofen, who gave me my first ski lesson.

Arthur Sandles

THE CALL OF THE SLOPES

It is one of those blue and white mornings which seem to crackle. The few dawn people in the village street give off breathy clouds into clean, cold air. Maids yawn their way to breakfast rooms which still await their first whiff of morning coffee. The snow has that crispness only seen in the first hours of light. The engineers start the first cable car run a few minutes behind time. They too have spent most of the night before eating, drinking, dancing and romancing.

In the first cable car are the real addicts. To leave warm beds, and all that they hold, to go to the top of a mountain at the crack of dawn after a carnival night suggests some sort of madness. Out of the cable car and into the chairlift to continue a silent drift up towards that blue, blue sky with hands tucked inside anoraks to ward off the freezing chill. And then the top. A few laughing exchanges in assorted languages . . . and on to the first run of the day.

Into the first hundred metres, a gentle thoroughfare of a *piste*. Time to settle down, time to discover that perhaps some of last night's brandy is lingering in the system. Over the brow of the hill into a waspish descent, furrowed and deeply mogulled on the outer edges by the less daring who had tackled it with long traverses and turns only when they became essential. The snow has a fine covering of morning powder. The skier weaves a pattern down the slope, the swish of ski on snow his only accompaniment. Then, a broad sweep as the incline eases, and into a mountain path. The trees beckon him into a Christmas-card tunnel of branches. Almost intoxicated he turns and finds himself in a gun-barrel—a smooth-sided half circle of icy *piste* which seems more like a section of the Cresta than a relaxing ski run. Bouncing off the sides, he emerges on to another broad treeless meadow. The speed rises and the rhythm flows.

This surely is the real joy of skiing. The zest of that joyful series of linked turns, the snow clouding up behind you in plumes, each tiny flake a little star catching its own share of the morning light. Later in the day the snow will lose something of this magic. The sun will steal a few degrees of cold away from the mountain and that bouncy powder will grow softer, more lethargic. Later on, those beds in the village will lose their last occupants who will take themselves unsteadily to the slopes. More laughter, more companionship—all offering delight. But there are times when selfish pleasure is peculiarly seductive.

At the bottom of the slope there is breakfast. Hot coffee, rolls or croissants fresh from the oven, a little cheese or cooked ham. And, perhaps, glances of mixed admiration and sympathy for such early morning madness.

Skiing is one of the most compelling sports man has been wise enough to invent. Perhaps ski resorts should be hung with notices reading: DANGER—SKIING IS ADDICTIVE. The person who first talks you on to skis could be giving you a 'fix' of something which you will need regularly for the rest of your days. In the early 1970s there were more than twenty million regular skiers in the world: that's the kind of figure that doesn't register—until most of them appear to be in front of you as you wait for a ski lift. Approaching half that total live in Europe, slightly less in the United States and Canada, with Japan rapidly catching up. These skiers find their pleasure in the great ski areas of the world, areas with names of magic. The Alps, land of St Moritz, Zermatt, Val d'Isère and Kitzbühel . . . the Rockies, where the powder snow lies deep and alluring at Aspen, Vail, Taos and Park City . . . Chile, New Zealand, Australia, Scotland, Norway (land of that old pastime and new vogue, the *langlauf*), Spain and, well, a dozen other countries. Both Austria and the United States boast almost one thousand ski resorts each, ranging in facilities from single drag lifts to multi-million pound complexes with hotels, apartments, night clubs, restaurants and miles of prepared runs bull-dozed over mountain sides, supplied with artificial snow when nature is a bit sluggish, and floodlit at night to give the dedicated an extra few hours on the slopes.

But skiing is not millions of people, concrete hotel blocks and attractive investment. To ski is to be free. To sail gracefully, smoothly and silently with matched pace and ease. Skiing is neither Kandahar, the exclusive club in Switzerland, nor American hot-dog racing. Skiing is to sweep down a slope of new snow with laughter in your heart, to share the delight of a spring mountain morning, to down a beer and munch a sausage while plans for the rest of the day are laid. Skiing is to dance the night away in some smoky cellar, exchanging loving glances with your companion, because glances may be the only part of each other's language you really understand. Skiing is snow, glühwein, hot chocolate, furry boots, fondue, brandy, moguls, tumbles and giggles. To ski is to forget that it can be cold, occasionally wet, that boots can fit badly and that you are not really as fit as you thought. To ski is to have your mind concentrated wonderfully; all you can afford to think about is the next turn your skis must make.

Skiing has been around for a very long time. In 1929, peat cutters digging on an island off the Norwegian coast found an engraved rock. The figure of a skier on that rock had been etched more than four thousand years before. Not that skiers in those days, or even in the relatively recent past of seventh-century China, were skiing for fun. There was no other way of moving at a reasonable speed over terrain unsuitable for animal-drawn sleds. Hunters in such circumstances were faced with the need to store food, retreat to lower valleys, invent traps or starve. For many primitive men this range of options boiled down to just one other— learn to ski.

Skiing came late to the Alps of Europe. There had been intermittent attempts to introduce skis to these mountains, but without much success. For thousands of years the inhabitants of the Alps preferred to tuck themselves away in their villages in November, with cows in the barns and logs by the fires. At the start of the nineteenth century, when word about skiing was beginning to spread, they saw little need to change their habits. But in the region of Telemark, in Norway, a revolution was taking place which would change all that.

Telemark: that's one of the key words that can vault across language barriers and establish you as a person of quality among the old timers in the bars of St Anton (Tyrol), Klosters (Switzerland) or Portillo (Chile).

For some years, the people of Telemark had been experimenting with a new style of ski. Even a skier today would recognise it immediately. With these new planks of wood, a traveller could go down a mountain in a series of straight runs across slopes, with awkward stumbles bringing him into a new line. But in Telemark, over the years, they were also developing ways of overcoming this awkwardness. The Telemark turn, a graceful one-legged kneel akin to a curtsy, cannot be done with a modern downhill ski binding, which fixes the heel of your boot to the ski. When Sondre Nordheim showed the beauty of his skis and the turn he and his fellows from Telemark had perfected, the people of Christiania, the ski heart of Norway in those mid-nineteenth century days, were astonished.

And that was the beginning of skiing for fun, and fun alone.

Since then, skiing has moved on quite a way. *Time* magazine reported that 1972 was the year that skiing passed golf as the sport on which Americans spend the most money. If you really become a ski enthusiast, there are plenty of ways of spending money, if you choose. There are plenty of ways of avoiding it, if you want to. You can change your skis as often as the ski manufacturers change the colour of their products—which is pretty often, as their eye for business glitters keenly—or you can keep them for as long as they last. If you are a recreational skier, taking a week or so on the slopes every year, those skis will keep you going for many a season. You can, of course, rent in resort areas, which is the best thing to do until you can pick your way around the maze of ski equipment. You can rent in Britain as well as in a resort—but confirm with your tour operator or airline in advance that they have room for your skis on your flight.

Getting to know the world of skiing is a great deal easier these days than it has been in the past. New teaching methods and new equipment have accelerated the transition from the huff and puff stage to sheer pleasure. Using short ski methods, it is possible to be doing those much admired parallel turns within hours, and doing them on the same *piste* as the rest of the jet set within days. Longer ski methods will leave you feeling more awkward at first, but provide a ground experience which will prove indispensable when you move to the exhilaration of skiing off the beaten track. Remember, it is not good business for either resorts or the ski industry as a whole to slow down ski tuition. The more people who are hooked on the pastime, the wider their smiles. So everyone wants to learn quickly.

Skiing today is an enormous business. Throughout the world, especially in France and the United States, massive amounts of cash have been spent on erecting purpose-built ski resorts. Ten million pounds buys a modest resort, but even then it takes a little while to get the money back. But back it comes eventually, sweeping in like the flakes in a December wind. The return comes initially from property, since most of the newer resorts are based on property development. After that, there is revenue from hotels, shops, restaurants, parking and, of course, the ski lifts. An effective ski lift system is the key to any successful resort. And he who owns the lifts, controls the skiers' crock of gold. Unfortunately, some of them know that and exploit the skier.

But that's a small piece of grit in the skiers' eyes. Ski resorts are the last citadels of relaxed and healthy holidays. You have the chance to either let go and enjoy it or push yourself to the limits of your ability. You feel the exhilaration of challenge, the exultation of cool air on your face, smooth snow beneath your skis, scenery sweeping past, joy in your own skill. Both the partnership and the contest are between you and the snow. It is not like cricket or football . . . you are fool or champion mostly to yourself. On a ski slope the world is yours. Back in the ski lodge no one can tell the difference between Jean-Claude Killy and the complete novice.

When to go

I suppose I have rarely been so drunk. There we were, two Englishmen in a Swedish car, picking an uncertain way through an icy mountain road in the Tyrol. At each village we had to call on several hoteliers. My companion worked for a tour operator and I for a newspaper. My unlikely assignment was to find out how tour companies negotiated their rates with resorts and what each partner in the deal expected from the other. The secret emerged very quickly: what each side wanted was several glasses of good strong liquor. The hotels and guest houses in those Austrian mountains grew prettier and prettier as first the day and then the evening wore on. We drank 'Hullo', we drank to the deal, and we drank 'Auf Wiedersehen'. By 2 a.m. we had fallen through the snow into the Whisky Mühle night club in Söll, one of the three most popular resort villages for British ski package tourists. Many a marriage has been made, and many broken, in Söll, although some ski *aficionados* turn up their noses at a resort with such middling skiing. Absent-mindedly, I muttered that even through my alcoholic haze I had noticed that the snow was a bit thin outside. The atmosphere froze. Then came that classic phrase known to all travellers: 'Ah, well you should have been here last week.'

Ski resorts, almost as much as sun resorts, rely on the weather. I say 'almost' because once the snow *has* fallen it is days, and often weeks before any more is necessary. It therefore pays to choose your resort with care, remembering the time of year you intend to ski and the sort of skiing you want to do.

In Europe, snow conditions in the first three seasons of the 1970s were erratic, and to escape to the deep snow of the American Rockies was a welcome relief. For two of those years the weather seemed to sweep up from the south, cloaking the mountains to the north of Milan with so much snow that it was embarrassing at the time. Mark Heller, Britain's most articulate, prolific and accomplished ski writer, has an appealing theory about ski weather. He reckons that if the first reports of snow and icy winds come from Rome or North Africa, skiers would be well advised to book for the

Pyrénées, the Aosta Valley, France or Spain. Places to watch for more northerly resorts are the Jura, Zürs and Kitzbühel. Whether this theory works or not the problem of spotting the right conditions is not easy, particularly if the cost of 'infallible' resorts, like Tignes or St Moritz in peak season, is beyond the family pocket. Basically, skiing takes place on the alpine meadows that lie between 900 and 2,500 metres in Europe, New England, Australia and New Zealand, and somewhat higher in the dry air of Colorado, Utah and New Mexico. If you pick the middle of the season, say February in the northern hemisphere, it has to be a terrible resort or a very bad year for there to be too little snow to ski. The earlier or later you go—pre-Christmas or around Easter—the higher you should aim. It is possible to ski in superb Christmas snow at 800 metres but it is wiser to make sure that there are at least a few ski runs starting nearer the 1,400 metre mark. Increasingly in North America, and to a lesser extent in Europe, resorts are installing artificial snow-making equipment which ensures that at least a few ski runs are available whatever the weather.

Skiing early in the season, Christmas and New Year apart, means less crowded conditions, smaller classes in the ski school, lower costs and the absence of families. It also means shorter days (and the delights of longer nights!), lower temperatures and per-haps a greater chance of snow storms and poor visibility. Later in the season, there are those long sunny days which may provide a suntan but sometimes mean well-worn, sticky ski slopes. Resorts tend to be more expensive in late February and March and con-siderably more crowded. It's at this time that local families usually take their winter sports break.

For ski resorts it is December snow which is important. It gives the slopes the firm base on which the main falls of January can build to provide the ideal conditions for the weeks of skiing to come. And the better the base in December, the more likely the resort is to have snow still on its runs in March. Go higher, and reliance on the weatherman is less important. At 3,000 metres and more, skiers the world over can enjoy themselves all year round. If you are *that* keen, there is no reason why you should not ski on Midsummer Day.

But beware of choosing a resort on height alone. The situation is complicated because climate does not conform to man's idea of an ordered world. Low-lying villages can snatch a little pocket of superb snow conditions, and high ones can be wind-blown at times. The other disadvantage of the very high resorts is that, in Europe at least, the tree line is around the 1,800 metre mark. Ski terrain without any trees at all appeals to many enthusiasts but is too bleak and bare for others. To start a run among the mountain peaks is a fabulous experience, enjoying as you do a god's view of the valleys below. But it is down among the trees that the real skiing is to be found.

Most of the resorts used by the better tour operators have reasonable snow records; otherwise the tour operators would be out of business. If you are booking late, or travelling independently, most of the 'quality' daily papers in Britain carry daily ski condition reports throughout the season. If you are a member of the Ski Club of Great Britain you also have access to the club's extensive information facilities. In the United States and France, radio stations in the ski resort areas give constant reports on snow conditions and on the conditions of the roads leading to the slopes.

Sadly, the best rough guide is usually price—in a particular area, at least. If you spot a resort which is cheaper than the others in the same district, there is often a good (or perhaps bad) reason for it. And if the price rises as you near the first week in March, it is simply because that is the time of year when things are right for recreational skiing. The *piste*-basher may prefer the air a little colder but those who enjoy some sunshine with their snow have to wait a few weeks. Pick a time which provides your mix of money and weather, remembering that the off-peak times generally mean fewer crowds and an absence of that curse of the ski slopes, lift queues.

Pre-ski preparation

A great deal of nonsense is talked about pre-ski exercises. It all sounds so frighteningly sporty or agonising. And yet when it comes to the crunch, the trim secretaries of Birmingham and the paunchy executives of London and Paris get up to such athletic, ski-village pastimes as catch their fancy without much apparent harm. So are pre-ski exercises necessary? Well, absolutely necessary, no; useful, yes.

The main object of pre-ski exercising is to clear the lungs a little, and tone up the necessary muscles so that the first few days on the slopes are not too much of a shock to the system. And the more fit you are, the less liable you'll be to twists and sprains. To prepare yourself properly, you should spend ten to twenty minutes a day doing the exercises, for a month or six weeks before you go skiing. If you *can* do this, you'll certainly enjoy your skiing more.

But if you prefer not to subject yourself to a routine, at least try to get as much normal exercise as possible. Give up using lifts (I live in a seventh-floor flat and do not always practise what I preach), and stop using buses or cars for any journey of less than a mile. Avoid over-indulgence in hard liquor and go easy on high calorie foods. It might mean cutting out a lot of the good things in life, but those that are left will seem more pleasurable. The plain fact is that if your muscles are toned up, you considerably reduce the already small prospect of injuring yourself. Strained knees or ankles can be irritating and can even ruin an entire holiday.

The muscles you want to improve with conventional exercises are in the thighs and the front and rear of the lower leg. After months of normal non-activity there is usually a need for loosening up the hips as well. And, certainly for first-timers, some work on the shoulders is helpful because in spite of all the contrary advice you will probably use them a lot. So what do you do?

It is almost unnecessary, surely, to say don't overdo it. However, it is a failing peculiar to the male to feel the need to punish himself for his own lack of fitness. This leads to a determination to show that he can still achieve at thirty-five what he could do at eighteen.

So he struggles through half a dozen press-ups . . . and can hardly move a muscle the next day. The more logical woman tends to operate with a self-imposed limit. This phenomenon demonstrates itself on the ski slopes as well—or at least it did until ski teaching methods improved. Men were content to battle alone with uncomfortable boots and stiffening limbs because in some way they felt their virility challenged by the obstacles. Until recently, there was a fairly high drop-out rate, particularly among non-teenage women. There is still evidence of this on the slopes, with men predominating in the thirty-plus ski group.

The first task is simply loosening up. A few minutes jogging will do this and you don't need more than a square foot of space in the bedroom or bathroom. As you begin to feel a bit healthier you can start running on the spot, raising your knees as close to your chest as you possibly can. Then stand still and lean over sideways, first right and then left, trying to touch your knee—and below it if you can—with the tips of your fingers. Do not let your body incline to either the front or the back. Do that four or five times each way, increasing it to twenty or thirty times when you feel ready for it.

Crouch on the ground, and then stand, using only your legs to lift you. Do that half a dozen times, again increasing the number of times you attempt the exercise according to the way you feel. If you think that is too easy, try it on one leg. You'll probably fall over unless you have steadied yourself with a chair.

Press-ups.

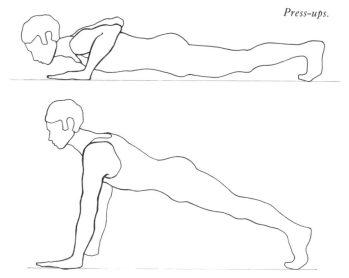

Lie on your back on the floor and do that old exercise of putting your feet under the bed and raising your shoulders off the ground, to tighten up your stomach muscles. I'm not sure this does much for your skiing, but it will certainly make you look a great deal better in tight ski pants!

Do try a few press-ups, but once you can do ten or more they start to get boring. Remaining in the press-up position, you might then attempt to launch yourself from the floor and clap your hands before catching yourself as you descend to the ground. This will smarten up your shoulder line, make your skiing more fluid, help with those long walks to the ski lifts carrying skis on your shoulders, and provide you with an impressive party trick for those long boozy evenings in the beer keller.

One of the accepted tests of whether you are really fit for skiing is to sit against a wall without a chair, with your thighs parallel to the ground. The strain on the thighs is considerable and you are quite strong enough for the slopes if you can hold that position for forty-five seconds or more. But unless you intend to be a ski-racer, I think it has limited value as a ski exercise. You can't do it for long enough for it to have any long-term effect.

Wall-sitting.

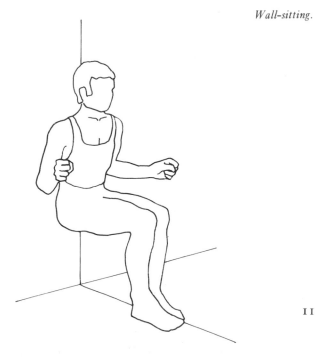

These days, increasing emphasis is being placed on ankle and knee flexibility in skiing. The more control you have over the movements of these joints and the more flow you can bring to your changes of weight and direction, the better you will ski.

A useful exercise for improving the muscles which control these joints is stair-hopping, something which you can do whenever you come across a flight of steps, but which might provoke some odd looks if there are spectators. Every time you come to steps, instead of climbing them in the normal way, put your feet together and jump up, taking a step at a time. Make sure your ankles and knees are together. To really get the feeling of being on skis, angle your feet with each step—first 45 degrees right, and then 45 degrees left. Try to keep on the balls of your feet and, above all, flex your legs to absorb your weight each time. Throughout the exercise keep your shoulders as square to the stairs as possible.

In that exercise, as in the next and in skiing itself, it helps to imagine all the time that you are treading on eggs. This is a favourite phrase with ski instructors, but it really does convey the message. Whenever you land, just try to think that too much shock on the ground will break the egg-shells, and seek to absorb that

Stair-hopping.

shock into your knees. Once you do this, and stop fighting the snow but simply glide over it instead, the whole thing seems much easier.

You can go a stage further with the 'stair-hopping' by jumping on and off a box, chair or low table. Stand sideways to the box and, with both feet together, jump up, sideways, on to it. Then jump down the other side. Repeat the process in the other direction.

Don't be over ambitious with the height of the box; eight or nine inches is quite enough at first and anything above eighteen inches begins to get too high. And beware. I've done this in socks on a polished bench and fallen flat on my face because it was all too slippery. Make sure you have non-slip surfaces.

All the other normal keep-fit routines are useful—touching your toes, rotating your trunk with arms extended, pull-ups and anything else you can think of. But don't take it too seriously. That is not what skiing is all about unless you aim some day to take part in the Olympics. You will probably think of ways of improving on the simple routine I have suggested. To quote that well-known Innsbruck skier and mountaineer, Otti Wiedmann: 'Gymnastics with a partner is usually fun and very useful.' Who would argue with that?

Chair-jumping.

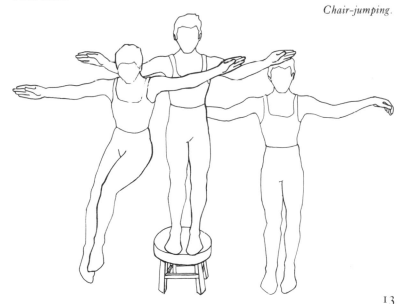

13

Artificial slopes

Recent years have seen a rapid rise in the number of artificial ski slopes in non-ski countries. These slopes are normally made of plastic and have the appearance of a nylon brush. This surface gives much of the feel of actual snow. It is marginally slower than snow, and a great deal more predictable. It is, therefore, superb for finding your ski legs, getting used to ski boots for the first time and eliminating an irritating remnant of stemming in otherwise perfect parallels.

Dry slopes are very much smaller than the real thing and unless there is a drag lift, which is rare, there is as much walking uphill as skiing down. Also, because of restricted space, the skiing is usually rationed. Normally, as the season gets into full swing, it is difficult just to drop into a dry ski centre and ski. You usually have to join a class or club or make sure you arrive at the times specially allocated for practice.

Ski without snow. Each winter part of Lord's cricket ground in London becomes a dry ski slope. There are dozens of similar slopes up and down the country, some of them open year round.

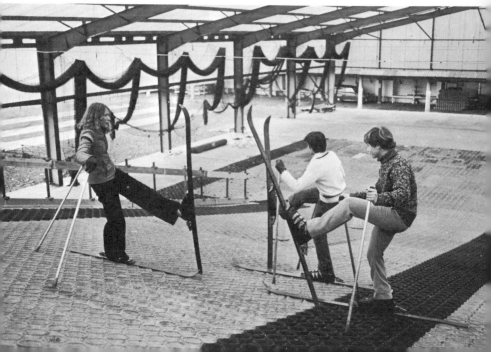

One enormous advantage the British dry slopes have for local residents is that the ski teachers speak English, or at least Scottish. If you are going skiing for the first time, half a dozen lessons on a dry slope will save several days of your actual holiday time. It is terribly important when you first ski that you know not only *what* to do, but *why* you are doing it. When you are being taught by an Austrian or Frenchmen who is having difficulty with your language, the whats are difficult enough to communicate, never mind the whys.

There was a time when experienced skiers looked down on dry slopes as something for novices only. As the slopes have improved, and teaching methods with them, so attitudes, too, have moved into sympathy with the whole idea, and now many very experienced skiers go to the dry slopes to keep fit and to improve their style. With ski techniques constantly changing this is very practical. A word of warning: even if the weather is mild, always wear gloves and long-sleeved shirts or sweaters. Dry slopes are not as soft as snow to fall on, and those nylon bristles can scratch exposed skin. If you already ski you might like to try grass skiing, using multi-wheeled and tracked skis. Since the technique is slightly different from snow skiing it is probably best not to try grass skiing before you've sampled the snow. In the U.K., the Ski Club of Great Britain will give further details. It's a much more popular sport than you might expect.

Equipment

Few sports provide more scope for argument about the equipment used than skiing. And, it must be admitted, skiers exercise the opportunity thoroughly; they enjoy the endless debates over the attributes of this or that ski construction, assorted boot styles, and the rival merits of different binding designs. If you are choosing equipment for the first time, you will find this complex and ever-changing world either baffling or fascinating, according to your turn of mind.

For those going skiing for the first time it is still best to hire equipment. There is an argument that rental prices have now reached a level that matches the cost of buying and then re-selling if you find you don't like either the sport or your equipment. The trouble with this theory is that to make the prices competitive you would have to buy skis which were so cheap and of such low quality there would be no re-sale value. In these days of rapid inflation it would be foolish to quote equipment rental prices, but the price of a better cinema seat will usually hire you skis for the day. Normally British tour operators sell 'ski packs', which can include equipment, lift passes and lessons. These will add about one-fifth to the basic cost of the holiday—but variations either side of that rough guideline figure can be considerable.

The basic rule for hiring anything is comfort. If you hire boots the first rule is: don't be pushed around by the shop staff. Above all, boots should be comfortable. If they pinch a bit, flop around a bit, rub your ankles or stop the circulation, ignore the impatient groan of the shop assistant and try some others. In the better boot shops, they'll sympathise and help. In the not-so-good shops, or even good ones during the weekend rush, there will be ill-disguised efforts to get you out of the store as rapidly as possible. When you say the boots are tight they will smile thinly and say they'll be all right when you've walked around a bit. They won't. Ski boots definitely feel different from normal shoes, but there is no reason why you should suffer agony because of that. It is a particular case where a visit to a dry slope before you leave for your holiday will help; there you can actually try boots to get the feel of them.

The same arguments apply to skis. There is a ski shop owner in . . . well, in a small Austrian village, who knows very few words of English. Among these few words is the comment: 'Ah! I think you are a good skier, I get you some very special skis.' The customer, flattered by the remark, takes whatever he is given! If you are a first-timer learning on the short ski, *ski évolutif*, or GLM method, you have less to worry about and probably little choice anyway. Just make sure that everything about the skis looks right, that there are no broken edges or loose screws on the bindings.

Even when learning by traditional methods, it is best to choose a ski on the shorter side. Skis are usually marked in centimetres. As a beginner you would have to be very tall and very heavy to need anything much longer than 190s. Skiers of more average dimensions would be happier on something considerably shorter. If it is your first time on skis, try to avoid a pair taller than yourself. Old-time ski instructors and ski shop owners might try to persuade you to take skis which reach up to your elbow when your arm is extended above your head. That's fine if you intend to go down the slopes in a straight line at high speed. Long skis give you stability at speed but they can be the very devil for turning. Until you become a competent skier, you will do yourself a great disservice by getting on to skis which are too long. It takes all the pleasure out of the sport. The ski shops will sometimes try very hard to push longer skis, often because there is a considerable demand for short skis these days and they are keen to get rid of all that old stock. Try not to be persuaded, but be ready to compromise in some European Resorts.

Having checked that the skis seem to be in reasonable condition —and remember that the sole and edges of the skis are much more important than the glossy top paintwork—pick them up. Some skis are disproportionately heavy, particularly low-priced and older wooden skis. Since you'll spend a great deal of time simply lugging the things about the village on your shoulder, it is worth reducing the load a little.

If possible, avoid skis with the old-fashioned cable bindings. Incredibly enough, these highly-dangerous attachments are still rented in many resorts. If a rental shop offers them, it almost certainly means that the skis themselves are several years old—and perhaps a little 'tired'.

Skis

Anyone interested in looking further into ski hire or purchase faces a fascinating world, and one which is changing constantly. Although skis look the same in outline from year to year, their construction and the materials used change frequently. Skis are designed to take you both through and over the snow. The more snow they have to go 'through', the softer the ski is, giving it flexibility to ride comfortably. Very 'soft' skis are used in deep snow. More rigid skis, designed to grip against well-compressed *pistes* or even ice, will tend to dig their toes into soft snow and can be difficult to handle.

Skis have a variety of attributes which are mixed to give you a ride suitable to your needs. Front flexibility is adjusted according to the snow in which you normally ski. For recreational skiing, you will most likely need something moderately flexible. Your ski shop will advise you, and most ski manufacturers produce very detailed specifications for their skis. The rear end of the ski is usually somewhat harder than the front. It is rear-end stiffness which affects your turning. Olympic champions will use skis which are so stiff you can hardly bend the rear end. To use that sort of ski for normal weekending and holidaymaking would be like trying to take the family for a run in a Grand Prix racing car: you wouldn't be able to handle it in traffic and everyone would get a bumpy ride.

When you place two skis together sole to sole you should see a gap between them in the centre. This bowed effect ensures that the ski is flat when your weight is on it. Without the arch the ski contact with the snow would be centralised and uneven. If the bow effect is small, and if it takes very little effort to flatten it, you will be skiing on the centre of the ski alone, making it extremely difficult for you to hold a straight line. If there is too much bow your weight will be concentrated at the ends of the skis, making it impossible to turn.

The recent development of multi-characteristic skis has made the whole business of ski choice appear more complex, but in fact it is safer. Almost certainly if you are buying your first pair of skis, and definitely if you are renting them, you should err on the soft side. The better 'soft' skis of today are fine for low speeds on the *piste*. It is turning quality that the intermediate skier requires. The moment the ski shop man talks about this ski being used by that national downhill racing team, it is time to say: 'No'. You can look good either in the hotel and on the ski lift with your super-hard racers, or on the slopes; take your pick.

You may also notice that skis have a slight 'waist' to them, and that the soles are not completely flat, but have a single groove running their full length. Both factors assist the performance of the ski enormously, producing a streamlining effect to ease the passage of the ski through the snow.

Skis are made from a variety of materials, and new ones constantly appear on the market. Most ski manufacturers use some combination of wood, plastic and metal, and employ laminations, fibre cords, honeycombs and a variety of other construction processes. Don't be wooed into buying a new model ski based on some completely new system until it has been on the market for at least one season. Ski equipment manufacturers have a habit of experimenting on skiers foolish enough to buy something because it is fashionable (and most of us fall for fashion at some time or another).

Wood is the oldest and still the cheapest material for skis, and is indeed the basis of many of the more expensive products. Wood tires quickly and all wooden skis can be distorted through misstorage. But wood has performance characteristics which are difficult to surpass with man-made products and is therefore often used as the 'core' of plastic or metal skis. But even all-wood skis are not just simple painted planks. Inside a wooden ski lies layer after layer of wood, the most favoured of which is hickory, bonded together in such a way as to equalise the pressures and provide just the right amount of flexibility. These wooden skis, like all others except cross-country models, will have a metal edge. This provides bite into the snow and facilitates modern turns, which would have been extremely difficult on the edgeless skis of yesteryear.

Experiments in ski construction produced a major revolution in ski design in the 'fifties and 'sixties when 'metal' skis swept the market. But even metal skis are not entirely constructed of metal. The revolution was brought about when a way was found to bind a laminated wooden core to metal strips. To read the books and magazines of the time one would have believed that these new and wondrous skis could transform any novice into a world champion overnight. What in fact they did was to make the American Head Company, which was the first to produce them, a world name to rival the great ski makers of Europe. Head skis became the status symbol of the slopes.

Sandwiching traditional wood materials between metal—a technique devised in Britain—gave the ski manufacturer much greater control over his product and the purchaser more confidence in his buy. Oddly enough, metal skis tend to be 'soft', which means they are particularly suitable for deep snow skiing and lower-speed turns. At high speeds, the skier finds the front ends of his skis tend to flutter like captured butterflies. This disquieting chatter, which can be dangerous on a fast *schuss* (a straight run) down a rutted track, is a major disadvantage. To some extent it is overcome on modern metal skis by the use of rubber inter-layers which provide a damping effect.

Metal skis are becoming more rare these days because of the greater manufacturing flexibility of the various plastics. There are, however, recurring experiments with metal-plastic mixes, mono-bloc construction and metal/fibreglass/wood laminates.

In the mid-1970s, plastic and fibreglass skis, still often with a wooden core, dominate the market, offering a broad range of prices in the middle to top bracket. There is a range of variations on the basic theme of compounds but the end result is a ski whose performance is almost mathematically predictable. The main difficulty with skis generally today, and with compound skis in particular, is that prices continue to rocket. The sudden rise in the price of oil-based products in early 1974 ended forever the age of cheap plastic. Overnight the developed nations of the world had to re-think the cost basis of their whole economies. The world ski industry, a substantial user of plastics, glass fibre and wood, was naturally not left untouched. The capital cost of regular skiing rose abruptly. The average price for a reasonable pair of skis now roughly equals the price of seventy-five gallons of petrol.

If you are intent on buying skis rather than hiring them, give it a lot of time and thought. There is little doubt that the best time to buy is in early spring. You will get very little use out of your skis that season but will have saved at least twenty per cent by buying at an end-of-season sale. There is, however, a danger in this: it can be a little irritating to have waited all winter only to find that the skis you had set your heart on have been sold.

Choosing skis can be something of an ordeal. Just as the range of equipment available to the skier is wide, so bees in the bonnets of ski shop staff buzz loud and persistently. Once you have made up your mind you may find yourself faced by a ski shop assistant who disagrees. Listen to him; he may be right. But beware the man or woman who will not in his turn listen to you, when you say why you have selected the skis of your choice.

Just as it is best to choose a ski which is made in such a way as to flatter your standard of skiing, so the need to go for the right sort

Cross-section and tip of ski.

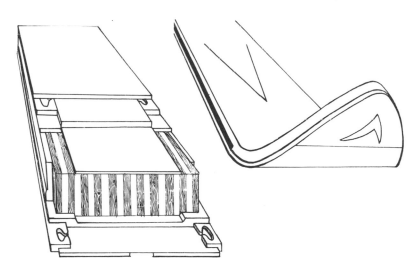

of ski length cannot be over-stressed. Once again fashion plays a strong hand in this game. Many of the ski school owners in the Alps are former champions who swept to success in races twenty years ago. They tend to cling to the philosophies which won them their trophies—and high on the list of their creeds is the conviction that the best skis must be a good six inches taller than the skier. In France and the United States this is now regarded as nonsense and even in the traditionalist heartlands of Austria and Switzerland the short ski is rapidly gaining ground. For the average recreational skier, particularly anyone over thirty, a ski which is above head height presents unnecessary obstacles to real enjoyment on the *piste*. Basically, however, you should ski on what makes you happiest. I have seen a pretty girl gleefully carving through very deep powder snow on 120cm skis—so short as to look little more than extensions to her ski boots, and certainly of the sort of length which would send a traditionalist into hysterics. With her was a man of, well let's say of more mature years, skiing as he had always skied, and probably always will, on giant 220cm planks. Both were happy and that is what skiing is all about. Fortunately the purists, ancient or modern, are losing influence rapidly.

Bindings
By far the most important part of any skier's equipment is the binding. This is the system which holds your boot to the ski. It is crucial that the binding should keep you in close contact with your ski at all necessary times and then quickly release you when it becomes essential. Since it is the binding and its adjustment that is the main safeguard between you and a broken leg, it is advisable to spend as much money as possible on getting the right sort of equipment; given a choice between economising on skis or on bindings, sacrifice the outlay on skis.

Bindings have progressed over the years from simple leather straps, through cable release systems—which are still to be found (and avoided) in some rental outlets—to modern bindings which, hopefully, can deal with most situations. The work that a binding has to do faces the designer with a considerable challenge. For example, it must be able to retain a firm hold on the skier as he goes fast over a bump, landing heavily and turning at the same time. But it must give way the moment there is any threat to a bone. The stress may come from a variety of angles—the skier can be thrown forward, backwards or sideways in hundreds of different positions.

The simplest bindings will usually handle a forward fall quite adequately. This is one in which the heel is wrenched out of the rear unit, if the bindings are properly adjusted. Normally they will also cope with a twisting action which takes the toe out of the front binding. Only the more sophisticated equipment can deal success-fully with a twist that takes the heel sideways to any degree. Various safety authorities in Europe and the United States test ski bindings and publish lists of approved equipment. Your ski shop can tell you which bindings have such approval, since the manu-facturers are usually keen to boast about it.

For the skier's enjoyment it is also very important that bindings should work simply. When you look at bindings in a ski shop, try to imagine what it is going to be like to adjust them, or step back

Binding releases.

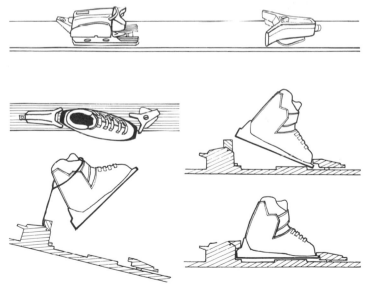

One of the latest examples of the classic step-in bindings which the average skier is likely to find on his rental skis.

into them, in deep snow and sub-zero temperatures on top of a windswept mountain.

Just as important as binding design is binding adjustment. It is nice to know that your skis will part company with your boots when the need arises. Particularly in the early days, when tumbles are a regular feature of ski life, it is difficult to resist the temptation to have bindings which are far too tight. Do resist. If you have a heavy fall and your skis don't come off, have the ski shop check them. If you keep falling and your skis come off frequently, re-strain the ski instructor who, particularly if he has a large class, will try to tighten your bindings and stop them coming adrift. This is only necessary if the skis are coming off before you fall or so early in any fall that efforts at recovery are in vain. Ask people who have had ski accidents why they had them and most will tell you that their bindings failed in some way, usually through poor adjustment. As someone who sometimes finds it extremely diffi-cult to stick to the rules, I have painful memories of falls when bindings have been too tight—usually in deep sugary snow when the ski stopped and I didn't. Or they have been too slack. The feeling of perplexed horror you get as you feel one ski come adrift from your boot at speed and perhaps even watch it zoom away with a will of its own before that inevitable tumble comes . . . that is an experience which should not be endured too often.

Bindings come in all manner of shapes, sizes and, these days, colour. Early season issues of the ski magazines will tell you what is new and occasionally offer lists of what is best among the old. Most bindings come as separate heel and toe units, but on the whole it is better not to mix brands. An alternative range of designs involves a complete binding unit attached to a permanent base plate. Your ski shop should have a selection of different types. The main rule to remember is that if you cannot understand how they work or how to adjust them in the shop, you will never do so on the slopes. Go for the best mix of safety and simplicity you can find.

All this applies to downhill skiing. Cross-country ski touring, a fascinating and growing pastime, is a different subject and is discussed elsewhere in this book.

Whatever bindings you buy or hire must have safety straps which keep the ski attached to the boot by a short life-line, or a ski-retaining device which will prevent the ski sliding off down the mountain if you lose it. And the word is *must*. In many countries and ski areas, a safety strap is a legal necessity, although sometimes, notably in the United States, a ski-retaining device is acceptable. Even if a safety strap is not mandatory it is certainly advisable. It

Bindings come in various designs and the skier's final choice is likely to be one of personal preference. The rotating heel binding (top) is very popular with fast skiers. Plate bindings in metal or extremely strong plastics are also currently enjoying a vogue.

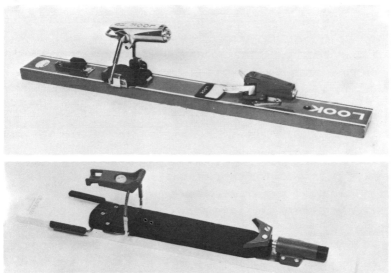

is infuriating to have to stumble down the mountain to find a ski which has gone off on its own; it is worse to find yourself with a massive bill for damages after your ski has hit some fellow skier further down the slope. A runaway ski can make 50 m.p.h. easily, and doesn't bother to avoid any obstacles, like human beings, which may be in its path. If your ski hits someone else you will normally be held responsible, however innocent you feel yourself to be.

Canting

One of the more recent rages in the ski world is canting, which is simply a new way of dealing with an old physical fault which none of us knew we had before. When we stand up, most of us do not have our feet perfectly flat on the ground, which means that our legs lean either in or out. Stiff modern ski boots accentuate this tilt which, in theory at least, has serious implications. It means that one edge of your ski will be pushed into the snow. Symptoms of tilting are the frequent catching of edges on the *schuss*, or your outside ski wandering off on its own as you turn. The cant is a wedge of plastic designed to compensate for the tilt, and effectively place your feet flat on the ground. Canting enthusiasts argue that it works miracles, as logically it should.

Unfortunately, translating theory into a practical application for the everyday skier is less easy. There are a variety of ways of testing for cants. Usually it involves standing on two pivoted foot-rests. Indicators attached to these rests reveal how far out of the perpendicular each leg is, and thus the amount of cant that is required. The problem is that different machines sometimes produce varying results for the same person, a fact which at least raises the odd question mark.

But canting is likely to be employed increasingly in skiing in spite of the present uncertainties, and there are signs that the cants of the future will be built into bindings or boots rather than sold as an optional extra. The cost of having your skis canted varies enormously, from just a few pence to several pounds, so if you are keen to have it done, shop around. The effect is likely to be as much psychological as real. I had my skis canted in 1973. While I felt better for it, I have serious doubts that it made any real difference to my skiing.

Sticks

Although most ski schools like their pupils to have their first few lessons without the aid of ski sticks, they are vital to your skiing once those first few steps have been completed. They will aid your balance, facilitate your turns, assist your developing rhythm, and help you to your feet when all that skill has still failed to keep you upright. Sticks are shrinking these days, with waist high being the trendy length at the time of writing. As every month seems to add or subtract an inch from the acceptable length, what you choose is a matter for yourself and your ski instructor. Using shorter sticks, your body will be pushed into a lower position as you bend your knees for a turn; otherwise, your sticks would lose contact with the snow. For the more modern advanced turns a shorter stick is essential since your bottom will be very close to the ground. If, however, you are a graduate of an earlier ski age, or prefer the ice-cool elegance of the Austrian classic stance, longer sticks are the thing. I feel that longer sticks are probably best for beginners because they help to stop the skier bending his body forward. Once he has learned the essentials of positioning, he can switch to shorter sticks.

A ski stick has a handle at one end, which has a leather strap attached to it. At the other end is a round 'basket', which is supposed to prevent the stick from sinking further into the snow than the few inches which the protruding tip allows. In fact, as a concession to modern manicured ski runs, the 'basket' today tends to be little more than a token piece of plastic. If you intend spending a lot of time off the beaten track it is worth getting bigger 'baskets'.

Most sticks today are made of steel or an alloy; you will occasionally come across wooden sticks and sometimes fibreglass. Metal is preferable for alpine skiing; it has greater durability than wood, and a better 'feel' than fibreglass. It is very easy to regard sticks as just an extra, and to pay little attention to them. But they will be with you throughout your skiing and must therefore feel right. Particularly important is that the hand grip and the leather

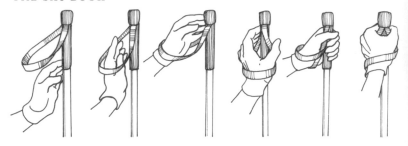

Stick straps.

strap, which goes over the wrist and passes up through the palm of your hand, should be comfortable. The strap should be either adjustable or of such a length as to fit securely on your wrist, but at the same time be easily removable when you use ski lifts.

Boots

There are two basic essentials in a ski boot. It should have a nice firm fit, and it should be comfortable. The firmness of the fit will give the skier direct communication between his feet and the skis, and comfort will enable him to enjoy that communication through long days of skiing.

Most boots today are made of some form of plastic. There are still some leather boots to be had, and they are alleged to be more comfortable in the long term. In the very bottom price bracket there are one or two rubber boots on the market. Plastic would seem to be the ideal ski boot material, however: it is completely waterproof and retains a permanent shape. Too much friendly flexibility in your boot means that you lose that essential contact between skis and skier.

It is how the plastic is used, and what else lies between the outer boot and the foot inside that is the subject of so much argument today. Most boots are of a straightforward plastic design, usually with five metal slips. The more advanced skier usually opts for a shell in which the outer part of the boot is a very stiff case which splits open to admit the foot and then clamps back tight around it. There are some shell boots for intermediate skiers, but in general terms the shell separates the aces from the rest of us mortals.

All manner of materials are used inside the boot to maintain comfort and warmth. Many skiers still stick to good old-fashioned fur, or some other natural padding material. If your feet do not have too many odd knobs and lumps on them and if you do not sweat a great deal, there is nothing wrong with fur-lined boots. Sweat will tend to mat the fur, and leave the boots with an evil smell.

In the early 'seventies there was a temporary passion for in-jected-foam boots, a trend which led to lines of boot buyers sitting patiently in chairs while assistants pumped chemical mixtures into a boot-liner sack. The mixture set around the foot, providing the skier with his own tailor-made foam lining. When the process was completed properly—and there are still some foam boots available—it was very satisfactory. Many skiers I know dread the day when they wear out their foam boots and have to buy something which they now regard as inferior. But foaming has many a pitfall. The process is not always done to the skier's satisfaction, and mistakes can be expensive. Once a boot is foamed, at least the lining, and more likely the whole boot, is useless for anyone else. Retailers objected to the amount of time involved in foaming and gradually the idea began to fade out. Oddly enough, the foam boot fashion, at its peak, caught on more strongly in Britain than in Continental Europe.

Foaming has now been largely replaced by flo-fit lining. In this case the boot has the same internal sack as in a foamed boot, but the sack is pre-filled with a thick, treacly substance which gradually melts with the warmth of the foot and moulds itself around the toes and ankles to give a nice snug fit. They are superbly comfort-able but one has to beware letting them get too cold before putting them on. Leaving a pair of flo-fit plastic boots in a car overnight can be a recipe for a troublesome start to the ski day as you wait for the treacle to warm up and the plastic to become flexible. I confess to being a flo-fit addict.

Ski boots have a rear shaft which is designed to support your lower leg in something like the correct ski angle. Obviously that angle will vary considerably from skier to skier, and particularly from skiing standard to skiing standard. In broad terms the faster and more aggressively you ski, and the more advanced your technique, the higher the rear shaft and the more acute its angle to the sole of the boot. This principle holds until you reach the most extreme stage.

There are some boots on the market which are impossible for normal skiing. In the beginner-to-intermediate stage of skiing you need a good firm grip on the couple of inches above the ankle, plus a degree of stiffness in the boot on either side of the ankle. Rear stiffness is of less consequence until you have improved. Indeed, putting a beginner in stiff, steeply-raked boots is likely to prove such a nerve-wracking experience that any eagerness for skiing would be instantly destroyed.

Moderately stiff boots are not dangerous—in fact they are less dangerous than the old softies—but the lack of flexibility in the boot means that your bindings must be carefully adjusted.

It is possible to obtain hinged boots, which allow for changes in the angle of your skiing; by adjusting the hinge near your ankle, you adjust your degree of lean.

Very approximately, boots cost around half to two-thirds the price of skis.

Anti-friction pads

As boot and binding design has become more sophisticated, designers have focused on ways to ensure that the laws of nature don't interfere with their basic tasks. The main culprit here is friction: although the boot is meant to slip easily out of a binding in the event of a severe fall, sometimes the frictional grip between boot and ski, perhaps aided by ice, snow or grit, prevents this. There are now dozens of pads on the market which you fit on to the ski, usually just under the ball of the foot. Most of them are faced with Teflon or some similar material, or have a mechanical aid, like discs or roller bearings. Some of the mechanical devices are prone to icing or seizure from grit. The Teflon pads are generally regarded as effective, but need to be kept clean.

Goggles and glasses

It is unwise to embark on a skiing holiday without some form of protection for the eyes. Anyone who has tried coming down a mountain in driving icy snow, or swinging down a *piste* on a bright sunny alpine day, will know the agony of attempting either without goggles or sunglasses.

Goggles should have as large lenses as possible and be comfortable. Never buy goggles without trying them on. They should fit snugly around your nose and at the temples. There must be side vents to lessen the possibility of misting up. Some goggles have double glazing and others have treated lenses. You can buy demisting materials, usually impregnated pads, in most ski resorts. Normally goggles have interchangeable lenses, one pair a bright yellow which will make things easier to see on dull days, and the other a greyish green which takes away the glare when the sun is very bright. If your dealer says the lenses are interchangeable, ask him to demonstrate this. Sometimes the supposed ease of changing is a myth. Some goggles today have a dual-purpose lens in them, which—surprise, surprise—is a greyish greeny yellow!

Later in the season sun glasses will be sufficient but you may need two pairs for different conditions. Lightly coloured polarised glasses are excellent for skiing.

Anyone who wears glasses faces problems. It is possible to get goggles which go over glasses, but often these are not very attractive. If you can spare the pennies it is worth buying prescription sun glasses, which are useful anyway during the summer months. Your optician will make these for you for only a pound or two more than normal glasses. Polarised prescription sun glasses cost a great deal more. If you ski regularly it is worth thinking about contact lenses, which will put you on a par with normal-sighted companions: your only problem arises from that dazzling mountain sunshine when you take your goggles off.

Clothes

As with all revolutions no one is quite sure when it really started. But certainly over the past few seasons the revolution in ski wear has been in full flood. Not long ago it was easy to say with some precision what you had to wear on the ski slopes if you were not to look foolish. Nationalities could be identified against the white background of the snow—the chic slenderness of the French, the over-long, over-large anoraks of the British, the brash sportiness of the Americans. Those days have gone. Today, in ski clothes as well as ski technique, anything goes. To some extent this is due to the fact that skiing is a younger sport than it used to be, and youngsters today are less willing to be constrained by the dictates of traditional fashion than were their forebears. But it is also the result of the growth of residential accommodation in ski resorts. Many resorts today have large numbers of apartments, whose owners regularly spend weekends and holidays by the slopes. These are not jet-setters. They are people who have saved their money and put it into bricks and mortar rather than stocks and shares. These ski regulars will happily enjoy themselves in old jeans and gardening sweaters—when the weather is right. So today at least you do not have to worry about fashion. If it looks good on the heath on Sunday afternoon, it will look good in St Anton in March.

But you do have to worry about other things. Even the most perfect snow can be cold, and sometimes wet. Even the world's greatest skier falls occasionally. Even the toughest of he-men is likely to get frostbite if he ventures on to a freezing mountain without gloves.

Anyone going to the ski slopes from a non-ski country will need to take an anorak, sweaters, ski pants, ski socks, gloves or mittens, headwear of some sort (preferably something that covers the ears), under-vests and long-johns. You will be able to ski in jeans and even an open shirt in some weather conditions, but if you are a holiday skier the chances are that conditions will change during your holiday. Be prepared. If you are a beginner you will definitely need water-resistant trousers of some sort, and ski pants are by far the best. Most jeans tend to hold the snow when you fall and it gradually melts through the cloth to your skin, a very uncomfortable feeling. Similarly, anoraks are ideal for skiing, not just because they look good but also because they are warm, light, waterproof, and generally made of some sort of anti-skid material that will stop you from slipping down the mountain every time you take a tumble. Skiing in good looking non-ski wear, faded jeans and garden shirt, marks you out as someone who must know what you are doing; and you can always cheat a little by spraying the whole outfit with a water-resistant treatment of the type sold to renovate old tents—a small piece of one-upmanship.

As for appearance on the slopes, it is worth remembering that bright colours look great against white snow. Something you think looks a bit obvious at home will fit in nicely in a ski resort. But try not to mix the colours too much. Remember that most of the time you will be skiing so well (!) that others on the slopes will only catch a glimpse of you swishing past. Mixing too many colours will simply confuse the onlooker. Long-term favourites on the slopes are red, yellow, sky blue, black and, more recently, murky chocolates, olives and burgundies.

The trend in anoraks today is to shortness and a close-fitting design—and in this unisex world these remarks apply to both male and female. Short anoraks, which end at the waist, are certainly much more comfortable to ski in than the traditional, bulky, mountaineering parka. However, they do have disadvantages. The slinky anorak has fewer and less spacious pockets and, unless you are wearing the right sort of trousers, they allow snow, wind and chill to get at your kidneys. I think the freedom of movement in the skinny anorak outweighs the disadvantages, but it is worth remembering the drawbacks if you are the sort of person who feels the cold badly, or likes to stuff a great amount of 'essentials' into your pockets. Whatever you settle on, it is important that the anorak should fit snugly at the waist. Many mountain-walking, or even fishing, anoraks are deliberately left baggy at the waist to allow an inner filling of warm air to build up. In skiing you move far too much and too fast for this to happen, and you need an elasticated waistband or a belt to help to keep the upper body cosy.

It is essential in all ski wear that you should be able to move as easily as possible. If, when you try on ski pants and anorak, you do not feel that you could play a game of tennis in them, think twice before buying them. A skier of reasonable standard burns five hundred calories in an hour of downhill skiing, and to do that he moves around quite a lot. If your ski pants are too tight, or your anorak too bulky, all that energy will go on producing sweat rather than giving you a great day's skiing.

As anoraks have grown shorter so ski pants have grown longer. There is usually an overlap of four or five inches between the top of the pant and the bottom of the anorak. This has remained constant, so that long ski pants designed for the trendy skier of today can come almost to chest level. At this stage they become dungarees and frequently have built in braces. Ski pants are made of stretch material and should be fairly close-fitting at the waist, hips and upper leg. This is not only comfortable but has the side effect of providing attractions for that splendid and much-practised alpine sport of bottom watching. The lower leg fitting of ski pants is an area of complete anarchy at the moment. You will still find traditional pencil-legged pants which tuck inside the boots. These are comfortable enough but tend to allow snow to get into your boot unless snow conditions are perfect or you wear special spats. More popular are 'flared' pants which came into fashion when flared trousers were the rage of the High Street stores, but stayed on the slopes after they began disappearing from the discothèques. Flaring, provided it is not too blatant, keeps snow out of your boot. In theory the flaring can catch on your skis but I have never seen or heard of this actually happening. 'Oxford bags' can doubtless be skied in, but I would not like to try it. The third sort of normal ski pant is that worn by most racers today. These pants have a fairly close-fitting lower leg which goes outside the boot (as with all ski pants there is an inner leg which fits into the boot and has a band that passes under the foot arch). There are slits at ankle level to allow access to the top boot buckle, although there are variations in the systems used. These pants combine the best of flared and traditional designs, but if you buy them make sure you try them on with your ski boots. The leg bottoms are not suitable for all types of boot, particularly those with a very high or bulky shaft. Racing pants usually have a stripe, normally of a contrasting colour, down the sides of the legs. This is not just for decoration. The material in these stripes is of a lighter and more flexible material, which allows the racer to have very tight trousers—and thus reduce his wind resistance to a minimum—but still be able to bend his legs. If you are tempted by racing pants remember that your ability may not be up to your appearance; if this is the case, it is like going down the slow lane of a motorway in a Maserati. Additionally, very tight trousers are cold. The racer only has to go to the top of the mountain (and is probably well wrapped up when he makes the journey) and then race down. You have to spend the whole day in your tight racing pants.

Not everyone, of course, goes in for the established anorak and ski pants outfit. Increasingly, one sees ski suits on the slopes. These are usually in dungaree style, made of proofed cotton or nylon materials, and extremely light. Suits and salopettes have enabled the designers to really get to grips with pattern and designs, in women's wear in particular. There are some superbly sexy outfits available, but while I am a great admirer of them I would hate to foot the bills that the most alluring of them present.

Sweaters serve two main purposes: they should keep you warm; and they should be presentable, since you will make most of your day-time social appearances in them. Take more than one with you, because sweaters tend to get a bit 'high' after several days' wear in a ski resort. Your sweater should be long enough both in the body and the arms not to expose areas of flesh or under-clothes to the elements, even in the most energetic of situations. In just normally chilly conditions you will need warmth around your neck, so your sweater should either have a roll-neck or be designed in such a way that you can wear a shirt under it which can be buttoned up if necessary. Most sports shops sell very practical cotton knit roll-necks. Alternatively you can carry a light silk scarf to tie around your neck if the weather turns nasty. If you insist on leaving your neck and wrists exposed you will certainly feel the cold much more quickly, a situation which could be dangerous if for some reason you had to spend a long time on a chilly mountain.

It is for this reason, too, that it is best to go for high-wristed gloves or mittens. Not only will the gloves keep you warm, but they will also stop snow creeping down to your fingers. For people other than the most seasoned alpine troops, it is virtually impossible to ski for any time without gloves. In any but the warmest conditions you would very likely get frostbite. I have been frostbitten once, when I slit a glove at the thumb without knowing it. It is an experience I would not recommend. It is extremely painful and recovery is slow; I had a painful thumb for well over a week. Whether you should buy mittens or gloves is a matter of personal choice. Gloves will give you much more freedom of movement but are less reliable for keeping out the cold, more so if they get wet. Mittens, particularly if you buy silk inner-gloves to go with them, will ensure hand comfort in any but the most extreme conditions. If you feel the cold, and are skiing early in the season, mittens may be best. As your skiing improves and you spend more time on the move you may prefer gloves.

Whatever you choose, *never* buy gloves or mittens that are made of plastic. The thin plastic material used for gloves tears very easily on boot clips and ski bindings. The gloves cool down and heat up very quickly, which means that when the weather is cold your fingers will freeze, and when it is warm your hands will be wet with sweat. Plastic gloves are about half the price of leather equivalents, but they are not even one-tenth the value. You will be lucky if they see you through two weeks of skiing and, unless you are very fortunate with the weather, those two weeks will be spent cursing your plastic gloves. These drawbacks are even more important with children's gloves.

Hats . . . well, who can say anything commanding about hats! As long as it will stay on your head, as long as it will cover your ears when necessary, and as long as it will either keep out the snow or not interfere with the nylon hood of your anorak (built in to pull over your head if conditions get really bad), it will do. What it actually looks like is entirely up to you.

Almost as important as the clothing you show to the public is what you are wearing underneath. Again, warmth and flexibility are important. Basically, you ought to be wearing a vest or T-shirt of some kind, and long-johns or tights under your ski pants. There are plenty of specially made long-johns available for the skier, but women's winter tights are just as good, half the price and suitable for both men and women.

Finally, there are socks. Years ago, when boots really were boots, socks had to be great lumpy things that felt like carpet slippers and, after a few days' wear, would stand in the corner at night and run to you by themselves when they were called in the morning. Modern boots have a snugger fit than the old models and are well insulated. The thinner the sock you can get away with, within reason, the more direct will be your contact with your skis. But flimsy nylon will probably be too cold and will do nothing to stop any chaffing there might be between boot and foot. Most ski shops sell good modern ski socks which are fairly fluffy on one side and smooth on the other, but are not too thick—remember, you should be wearing tights as well.

Après-ski clothes

Since a great number of people go most of the way to their ski resort by air, the problems of carting large quantities of baggage around have removed forever the idea that no well-dressed *après-skier* ever appeared for two evenings running in the same outfit. But . . . there are basically two types of resort, and two types of skier for *après-ski* activities. Some resorts do have very fashionable evening retreats, including theatres and casinos. And some skiers are dedicated to the night life rather than the slopes. If you choose a resort where there is an accent on evening activities—St Moritz, Gstaad—or where you are skiing from a large town—Innsbruck or Grenoble, for example—you may wish to join the jet set, and dig out the long dresses and dinner jackets. That is between you and the excess baggage charge (it is unusual for any excess baggage even to be allowed on charter flights). But even in the glossy resorts, the need for fashion-plate dressing is rare, and mostly you would find that you were grossly over-dressed.

Normally ski resort evening wear is completely relaxed—sweaters and trousers are the thing. You can *après-ski* in your ski

37

wear if you like, but you will probably find that ski pants are far too warm for the centrally-heated restaurants and discothèques of most resorts. For both men and women, average-weight trousers will be fine.

Remember when you pack whatever you plan to wear in the evenings that you are probably going to do some walking around snowy streets as you burn the midnight oil. It is for that reason that women should think twice about packing too many skirts or dresses. A skirt can give you a nasty chill in the village square as you stumble back to your hotel with the snow outside, and maybe a little too much glühwein inside.

The only insistent advice is on footwear. The accent in ski resorts is on practicality. If you pack those platform-soled or lofty-heeled shoes you will find that they either remain in the case or send you tumbling into some snowdrift. There are some quite attractive non-slip shoes and boots available in the ski shops and shoe stores. The ski shop versions are made for the job and tend to look better, but they do cost a good deal more than those you will find in the local shoe store. Big furry boots have remained a firm favourite in ski resorts for many years. They look super . . . but make sure you can tuck your trousers or ski pants into them, because they look dreadful if they have to be squeezed inside a trouser leg. Also remember that furry boots can get very dirty if the snow is at all slushy and wet, as it can be in some low-level resorts and indeed in all resorts towards the end of the season.

Generally, it is much easier to pack too many clothes rather than too few. Women would be better off throwing out a few clothes and packing a portable hairdryer (dual voltage and with a plug con-verter), because skiing can play havoc with your hair. One pair of trousers and a few shirts or thin sweaters will see you through most ski holidays. You can always ring the fashion changes with acces-sories, but aim for fun-style jewellery and belts rather than the flashy variety.

Life is even easier for men. One pair of trousers and a few drip-dry shirts will keep you going for months. Just make sure you have somewhere to put your money when you take your outdoor jacket or anorak off in a restaurant, bowling alley or discothèque.

Lotions and potions

Those high alpine valleys which are so tempting to you in the winter are inhabited year round by hardy farmers, who are usually to be seen in the winter months dressed as ski instructors and yelling 'bend ze kneeze' at passing classes. Their skins seem to have been made for the tough treatment of the mountain meadows but, male or female, yours probably wasn't. The main essentials, for both sexes, are a suntan lotion or cream of some sort, a lip salve, and a moisturising cream. The best-known brands aimed specifically at the ski market are probably the European Piz Buin range, and the American Bonne Belle.

The problem for most office-working town-dwellers is the extremes of conditions likely to occur on any mountain. Your skin will be pounded by unfiltered ultra-violet rays from the sun; brushed from time to time with snow; swept by occasional icy winds; and baked in front of open log fires. The suntan lotion is an obvious need, but buy something that is easy to apply and in a manageable container—a tube is probably best because you can carry it round the slopes with you if the sun gets really fierce. Be sure to buy a lip salve that is for cold conditions and not the sunny seaside; otherwise you will get to the top of the mountain and find that the salve is rock hard and would rip the skin off your lips if you tried to use it. At room temperature, the salve should be quite gooey. If you do not use a lip salve it will not take much cold sun to split the lips. At ski-run heights, the air is often very dry and licking your lips simply makes them worse. It is this dryness which makes the moisturiser important unless, of course, your suntan cream acts as a moisturiser as well. If a man shaves in the morning he will remove much of the natural moisture from his skin. Exposing such stripped skin to the elements can produce burning and flaking and will almost certainly make you feel colder than you need. The woman in your life should be able to offer a bland fragrance-free moisturiser which will make your skin happier and not interfere with your masculinity.

Women should remember that whatever make-up or beauty aids they wear will have to stand up to severe practical tests. Before you attach the false eyelashes and administer the blusher, remember you are about to spend a day on a cold and possibly windswept mountain—and may even be the target of some well-aimed snowballs.

You will also need a deodorant.

Accidents and insurance

There is no denying the fact that some skiers hurt themselves. Magazines must have entire filing cabinets stuffed with 'skiing accident' jokes. But the standing joke about healthy young people trooping off to the ski slopes to be brought back in wheelchairs is a long way from the truth. There are two main and easily avoidable causes of injury: poor or poorly-adjusted equipment, and a lack of fitness. Both these factors are accentuated by the tendency of many skiers, particularly younger men, to ski more aggressively and longer than they are really able to. Surveys indicate that the main source of mountain doctors' business is from younger people who have accidents towards the end of the day. Oldsters tend to know when they are beaten.

The damage caused in most accidents is not in fact a break, but simply twists and bruises. Often this is because the skier has not spent enough time doing pre-ski exercises. These tone up the muscles and help to ease the strain when you are forced into positions you never actually thought about before. If your muscles are slack, particularly around the knee, when you are having your first lessons, you will put all the weight on to tendons and cartilages which are really there as communications and buffers, not weight-carrying moving forces like muscles. So rule one is to do what you can to get yourself moderately fit for the slopes, rule two is not to push your luck, and rule three is to make sure your bindings are properly adjusted.

Statistically, one skier in a hundred ends up in hospital during his first week on the slopes. After that the danger rate falls rapidly. For this reason ski insurance for one month is not very much more expensive than for two weeks. The accident rate for ski school pupils is well below the average, and is even lower if short skis are used. But ski accidents when they do happen normally have the blessing of being relatively simple. It is highly unlikely that you will do yourself lasting damage on the slopes. You *may* break a leg, but this is most unlikely, and if you do it would probably be a clean break. You are a great deal safer on skis than on horseback and probably safer than you would be on a rugby field. And you are much more in control of your own safety on the slopes than you are in either of the other situations. The odds are against hurting any other part of your body than your legs, but be particularly careful when conditions are very icy.

It is a very foolish skier who does not take out ski insurance before going on holiday, and most package tour companies insist that you are insured. But remember that ski insurance only pays for treatment after an accident; it does not prevent the accident itself.

Ski insurance needs very careful examination, the small type included, before you sign the paper. You should be covered for three basic costs (quite apart from normal travel insurance against baggage loss or other mishap). These are medical expenses, including ambulances, your return scheduled air fare plus the fare of anyone who travels with you, and personal liability. Beware of a policy which splits the costs down into £100 for this, £50 for that, etc. You could be in a situation where you are flown down a mountain by helicopter ambulance, X-rayed many times by some local specialist, and then discharged as uninjured—the ambulance fees would be heavy. Similarly, if you only have simple fractures, but of both leg bones, you will probably be in the local hospital for two weeks, comfortable but frustrated. The fee could run to hundreds of pounds. Remember that, if you do break a leg, it may be that you will require two scheduled flight seats back from your resort area, one for you, and one for your outstretched leg. If you are badly hurt, you may need a nurse or a friend to travel with you.

Any insurance worthy of the name should cover you for medical and transportation costs, however incurred, to at least the level of three weeks' hospitalisation in a good class hospital at the area you are visiting. If the personal liability coverage, which is for any accidents you may cause but may not necessarily be involved in, is less than £25,000 look for another insurance company. You could easily swing a ski stick haphazardly in Switzerland, damage the eye of a passing skier and find yourself with very heavy damages indeed. A total of £100,000 is a more acceptable figure, and the cost of such insurance is relatively low. The main thing is to ensure that there are as few restrictions as possible.

If your ski insurance says 'no racing', as it almost certainly will, and if your tour operator says 'regular village races for the visitors', get a written undertaking as to whether or not you are covered. One thing to remember is when in doubt, don't sign. If you are uncertain about your tour company's insurance arrangements, do not hesitate to ask questions. Your travel agent or your insurance broker can also give you further advice.

It is worth finding out who picks up the bill if someone steals your rented skis. Rented equipment is usually excluded from normal ski insurance cover, but sometimes ski shops make the hirer responsible. You should enquire how payment is made in the case of a broken leg. One or two companies pay the hospital and doctors direct. Others indulge in the expensive process of making you pay the bills first and then claiming the money back. This is fine if you are the sort of person who can write a cheque for £500 without a qualm.

Otherwise, your medical problems are likely to be no more serious than they are at home. If you are subject to tummy upsets abroad, usually caused by a change in the chemical content of the water rather than some evil disease, then Diocalm is an excellent remedy. This is simply a variation of old-fashioned Morphine and Kaolin in tablet form. Take a small canister with you; the tablets will keep until the summer if you do not use them. Otherwise a few sticking plasters for the odd scratch, and some antiseptic cream would be useful.

In some areas, particularly newer ski resorts in relatively under-developed tourist areas, women would be advised to take their own supply of tampons. If your skiing is going to take you to a really way-out place, such as the Himalayas or some of the more remote parts of South America, pack some Puritabs. These are small tablets which chlorinate your drinking water. The water tastes as if it has come straight from the corporation swimming pool, but at least it is germ-free. If you expose yourself to too much alpine sunshine, then After Sun, or some equivalent lotion, will soon bring you back to normal and some Bonne Belle bronzer (a stainer), will transform that brilliant red into a golden tan until you recover your normal colour. I have never tried Sylvasun anti-sunburn tablets, but am told by those who have that they are very good.

The ski slope code

The first thought about skiing, that it must be a leg-breaking occupation, is to some extent confirmed by that initial view of the slopes. There they all are, falling about all over the place. Then, as you watch more carefully, you see that the falls are nowhere near as bad as they look. Even the hardest of snow is quite soft stuff on which to land. But accidents are caused by other things besides falling, and it is for this reason that there are certain rules of the road on all ski slopes. Most of them are just plain common sense. They are designed principally to avoid collisions which, although relatively rare, can be quite serious. If two skiers collide at, say, 30 m.p.h., a few bruises can result.

These are some of the basic rules.

Always ski in control. If you really feel you have 'lost it' to such an extent that you could not stop or turn if a crevasse were to open in front of you or another skier were to fall across your path, gently sit down to one side. It is highly unlikely that you will come to any harm by doing that.

Remember that the slower skier has priority. If you are overtaking someone it is up to *you* to make the right overtaking movements and not force the other person to pull over. Remember that the person ahead of you may not ski as well as you do, and may swerve suddenly, perhaps nervous about your approach. On a narrow trail try to give good warning that you are about to overtake, naming the side on which you intend to pass . . . 'on your left'. Quite often you will be skiing where you do not know the language, but a call of some sort is better than nothing. Some skiers attach cow-bells to their wrists and I have heard hooters on the slopes. The former are perhaps a little pretentious, and the latter clearly antisocial in the extreme.

If you hear someone behind you, whether or not they let you know they are there, make it easy for them to pass. You may have the right of way, but it is only polite to clear the path a little. Don't make any sudden movements, but pull slightly over to one side. On very narrow trails, beware of your ski sticks—they may be flailing about more than you realise.

Check before you start off from any standing position that the trail you are about to take is clear and that you are not going to get in the way of someone coming up behind you. Make the same check as you come off one run to another. Ski runs often cross one another and it is easy to shoot across the path of on-coming skiers without realising it.

If you have an accident, and feel that you might have done more than just bruise yourself, move as little as possible. If you can, raise your arm to attract attention and then just wait. In most modern resorts there are plenty of ski teachers and ski patrollers about and they will know what to do. If you are not hurt, get off the run quickly, or someone might ski into you.

If you see someone else who has had a serious accident, you must do two things. Take off his skis *as gently as possible* (unless this can't be done without substantial movement of the injured person) and place those skis ten to fifteen yards above the skier in the form of an 'X', upright and with their tails firmly in the snow. This will warn on-coming skiers that there has been an accident. Try to get assistance: wait for a few minutes for someone else to join you, so that one of you can ski down to a lift station to summon help.

It may be some time before skilled help comes, so if you can spare your anorak to give the injured skier extra warmth, do so. When you ski down for help, try to remember the location of the accident as exactly as possible. Unless you are accomplished at first aid don't try to move the skier. If simple common sense is not sufficient warning, remember that in some countries you can find yourself in serious legal difficulties if your attempt to move the skier causes further injury.

If, when skiing, you want to stop for a rest or to wait for a friend, never come to a halt in a position which obstructs the progress of others—particularly if you are just over the brow of a hill.

Never venture off the prepared runs unless you are accompanied, and never go a long way off them unless you know something about avalanches and weather conditions. If you *are* caught by an avalanche—highly unlikely in the ski resorts of today if you stick to the main ski areas—do your best not to panic. You may be able to help yourself by 'swimming' in the snow as it sweeps down, but that is going to be pretty difficult if you have not taken off your skis in anticipation. It is better to cover your face with your hands so that when you settle you will have an area of air in which to breathe. Immediately you come to rest move around a bit to maximise this space before the snow compacts around you. Skiers have survived for several days buried like this, so don't abandon hope. Shout from time to time to attract attention, but try to conserve your energy. If you see another skier being buried and then cannot find him yourself, mark the place clearly and go for help. If you do not mark the spot with a sweater or something—the larger the better—a search is almost certain to be fruitless.

The ups and downs of ski lifts

Some people are able to handle ski lifts, but for me they have always seemed to have minds of their own. They are growling contraptions of metal and cable which are intended to get you from the bottom of the mountain to the top. The jumbo cable cars and mountain railways are fine, but the drag lifts, chairlifts and Pomas always appear to be moving at a rate either slower or faster than I have anticipated. The only comfort is that the first few yards are the worst.

In any ski resort you will need a lift pass unless you are skiing cross-country. If you have bought a package tour this pass may well be included in a 'ski-pack' along with ski rental, but if not you will find that the ski pass, or *abonnement*, will be one of the major costs of your holiday once you have arrived. It therefore needs some thinking about.

Basically you should not over-buy. In other words, if you have never stepped on skis before it is a waste of money to buy a full week's pass for every lift in the valley. On the other hand, at any standard of skiing it is a mistake to buy one-trip tickets, which simply take you up to the top of a run. The cost of a day of even moderately active skiing, if you buy tickets in this way, will horrify and financially cripple you. These one-trip tickets are not really intended for skiers; they are for spectators and summer visitors who simply want to go to the top of the mountain to walk around.

If you join a ski school, or have a private instructor, you should get advice on what is the best sort of ticket for the lessons you are likely to have. There are three basic types of tickets: passes for a period of time (afternoon, day, three days or one week); passes for a number of rides (usually in the form of a point card—each journey will cost you two, five or ten points and your card will be valid for, say, one hundred points, with attendants punching out the points as you take the rides); and one-trip tickets. For the beginner who has not been given a full pass as part of the package, it is probably best to get a point card of some sort. The cards are rarely dated and are transferable. This means you can use the points over several days and you can share a point card with a friend. Once you reach a measure of competence it is time to look at the full *abonnement*. The longer the period of pass you can buy, the better. Often for a three-day pass or above, and sometimes even for a day pass, you will need a photograph. Most resorts have facilities which provide passport-style photographs quite cheaply and in some the picture is part of the cost of the pass. Always enquire at your hotel about where to buy lift passes. Sometimes they are not available at every lift station (this is particularly true of the longer passes). It is irritating to have carried your skis half-way across a village only to find that you have gone to the wrong place to buy tickets.

When skiing you will come across all manner of lifts, but on the slopes they will usually fall into three broad categories—gondolas, chairs and drag lifts. To reach ski *areas* you may find yourself riding in a mountain railway or a cable car, which is simply a large container holding upwards of thirty people at a time. Neither of these presents any particular problems of technique, except perhaps *après-ski* technique, since a crowded cable car is a splendid place to start a conversation.

One down from a cable car is a gondola. These are small bubble cars which normally hold four people. They are used for high-density, long-haul journeys and are probably the most comfortable and sociable way of going up a mountain. The bubble has large perspex windows and you can enjoy magnificent panoramic views as you make your journey to the top. People using gondolas do not wear their skis; they place them in ski carriers which are outside the cabin itself. It is best if your skis are strapped together for the trip, not because they would fall off but simply because you will find it easier to get them in and out of the container. Usually you carry your ski sticks with you inside the cabin, but some ski lift companies insist that these, too, must be placed outside. The gondola doors open automatically as it approaches the departure platform and close again, or are closed by the attendant, as the ascent begins, so there is no need for the skier to do anything except place his skis in the carriers and climb inside.

The next thing you are likely to meet is the chairlift. For this you would normally wear your skis, but sometimes conditions at the base station are not good enough and your skis will be placed on separate seats by the operator. Chairlifts move quite quickly so it is important to be correctly placed as the chair approaches. You take your ski sticks into one hand and leave the other free to hold the chair as you sit down. Always look behind you to watch the chair coming. Chairs, whether single or double, are supported by one central column, or by two outer columns attached to the arms of the chair. Always look over your shoulder at the approaching supporting column: if there is a central support, look inwards and

Chairlift.

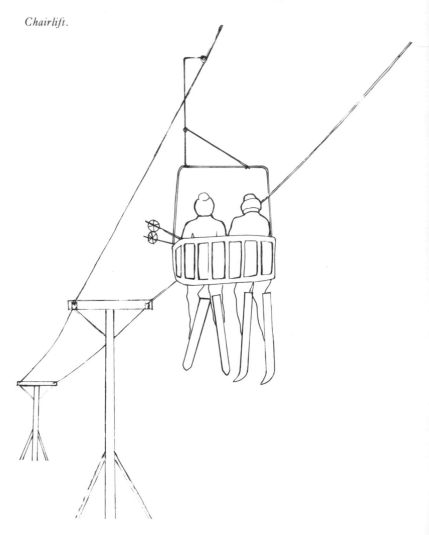

carry your ski sticks in the outer hand; if there are outer supports, look outwards and carry your sticks in the inner hand. It is important on any lift to keep your skis in a straight line as you start. Falls at the start of a chairlift are rare, and are usually caused by skiers not realising that the chair is moving quite so fast, but it is a good habit to keep your skis straight anyway, because on drag lifts disaster will strike unless you do. Leaving a chair is simply a matter of sliding off the seat and walking away. Make sure you remove the safety bar or chain some fifty yards or so before the end of the lift—which will give you time if you get it caught up somehow—and also keep the tips of your skis slightly raised as you approach the landing platform so they don't dig into the snow and tip you off forward. Most chairlift arrival platforms are flat, and therefore you must shuffle away in the direction indicated either by arrows or by the lift operator. Get out of the way as quickly as you can, or you may get some strong words from the operator; if you become an obstacle to the skier behind you the operator will have to stop the lift. Sometimes chairs have sloping arrival areas and you find yourself sailing downhill from the moment you dismount. This is not half as dreadful as it first sounds; the post-lift slopes are usually short and gentle. If your instructor has let you use the lift he is confident you can get off the thing.

Much more trouble is caused to the beginner by drag lifts than by chairs. There are two main types of drag: the T-bar, in which a cross bar is used to bear your weight as you hold on to a central cable, and a Poma lift, which has a tea-plate sized disc on a central metal tube which you place between your legs. In both cases the crucial points to remember are to keep your skis together and pointing straight, to carry your sticks in one hand, to gather yourself together as much as possible before take-off, and to relax. If you are not relaxed it is likely that there is very little 'give' left in your body, so that when the drag lift starts to pull, the force can tip you over. With a relaxed body you will absorb the initial pull comfortably. Unfortunately the pulling force of a drag lift varies considerably from lift to lift. Some will gently ease you away from the start, and others will literally lift your feet from the ground. Getting yourself together means assembling your skis, sticks and limbs in the positions they should be for the start. Try to avoid bending forward and sticking your bottom out. Since the force of the lift is directed at the seat of your pants, a forward lean will simply rocket your whole body straight ahead as if you had received a kick in the rear. If you are in a more upright position the force will bend your body like a bow at first and you should remain in control.

T-bars are difficult to get used to at first, but it is merely a question of balance; once you have done it a few times you will realise it is not such an alarming experience. Whether riding in pairs or alone (it is best at first to travel with someone who knows the way to ride a T-bar), you rest on one arm of the T, with your inside arm grasping the central bar firmly at shoulder height. Use your other hand to hold your ski sticks and to steady your position on the T-bar. You can ride a small T-bar solo with the T between your legs, which is much easier, but if it is a big two-person drag lift a beginner riding solo might find the process of getting off rather tricky.

Poma lifts have one long tubular aluminium bar with an inverted question mark at the end, finished off with the plastic tea plate. You normally have time to take up position and place the plate

T-bar.

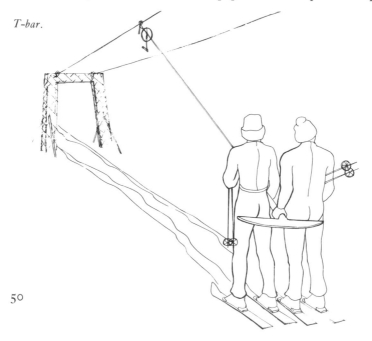

comfortably before the operator trips a release mechanism which sends you soaring, sometimes with some violence, up the slope. Occasionally the way the lift has been built means that the positioning, the release, and the take-off are all meant to be in one smooth movement. If you fall on the first attempt, don't worry. Large numbers of people do, and hopefully it will mean that the operator will give you more sympathetic help next time. Before you make that second attempt make sure you are not being rushed . . . take it easy . . . and check above all that your *skis are together and pointing straight up the slope.*

On nearly all drags you will end your journey on a slope. In the absence of signs to the contrary, if you are riding a T-bar with a companion, decide which way each of you is turning at the top (usually you will be going the same way), and which one of you is going to 'cast off'. This would usually be the person on the outside of the turn you are about to make. He will hold on to the centre bar firmly while his companion gets off, and then push the bar aside and ski off the track himself. With a Poma it is only a matter of sliding the disc down and out through your legs. The pulling force of the lift will carry it clear. Only get off lifts where you are told to do so. If you fall from a lift while it is travelling, try to get off the track as quickly as possible.

Poma lift.

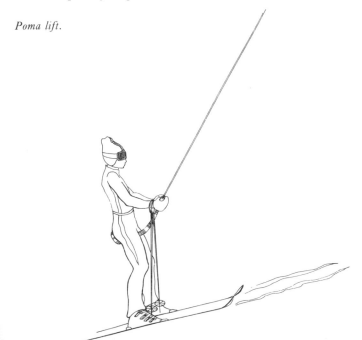

THE ROAD TO SKIING

The best part of the first day in ski school is the hour in the Weinstube after the lesson. Then you can laugh about the instructor's English, your companions' ski ability, and your own incompetence at handling the lesson of the day. You will rapidly become armed with ski school jokes. As you fall flat on your face and sprawl waiting for the ski instructor to help you up, a heavily-accented voice will call across the snow, 'Hey, eet iz too early for zee flower pickings, get up pleez'. I recall seeing a pretty girl struggling in vain to do her parallel turns, and being told gently as she fell for the tenth time: 'Remember this about skiing, my dear. As long as you keep your legs together you will never be in trouble on the slopes.'

In recent years the whole business of ski teaching has become somewhat confused, as tuition methods are under constant review. At the upper levels of the ski world there is some agreement on how newcomers to the sport should be treated, but different countries take differing attitudes, and you will find many a ski instructor who is ploughing a personal furrow. The ski tuition described in the following pages is not necessarily the *best* method, but it is what you will come across most frequently. It is all very well to talk about *ski évolutif* and the most advanced techniques of short ski tuition, but it is most unlikely that you will be presented with these methods in the Pyrénées or Bulgaria—or, for that matter, in Austria.

Basically, if your instructor is good it really doesn't matter what line of ski instruction he follows. In the medium-to-long term, most types of ski instruction will get you to the same standard in the same amount of time. In the early stages, tuition on short skis will make you a parallel skier more quickly, but traditional long ski methods will give you all-round ability. On balance, most experts plump for the short ski methods for the recreational skier. These methods, and there are more than one, will certainly give you a more enjoyable introduction to the sport; they will not necessarily make you a better skier in the long run.

If you switch from one ski area to another and your new instructor attempts to make you unlearn the techniques you have acquired earlier, you will run into difficulties. The only way of overcoming this is to try to go to resorts which have the same broad ski instruction theories for at least two years running. After that, you will have the confidence to fight your own battles.

Whatever technique is used, if you are a normally fit ski beginner—and that is simply someone who can play two or three sets of tennis without suffering complete exhaustion—you should be coming down the easier long runs from the top of the mountain after three days, and skiing with joy and some confidence (or perhaps confidence and some joy) after a week. In two weeks you will be a fully-fledged member of the ranks of recreational intermediates which, if you pause to look around, you will realise is the peak standard for most of us.

We will turn to the various ski school techniques in a moment but, whatever school you learn in, there are two basic rules for skiing. Remember them and you will be able to ski any mountain— in time. If you fall on the *piste* when no physical obstacle has come across your path you will probably have broken one of them. The rules are:

1. *Keep the upper part of your body away from the mountain.* This is the most difficult lesson to learn. Your every instinct will be to lean into the mountain. Do that and your legs will slip from under you. Look down the mountain as you traverse, look down the mountain when you turn, look down the mountain when you stop.

2. *Bend your knees.* This is the cry you will hear throughout the Alps, the Pyrénées, the Rockies and the Bugaboos. It means what it says. Do not bend your waist, or your neck . . .

but your knees. With bent knees you can absorb bumps, flex quickly into instant turns or come to a rapid stop. Keep your knees straight and any simple jolt will send you tumbling. There will be times when the instructor yells at you . . . and you will growl under your breath about injustice because you think your knees are bent. Often, in fact, the skier is simply bending his whole body into a crouch, which is a recipe for disaster.

Starting the Day

Ski school in most resorts starts at 10 a.m. and runs for two hours in the morning and another one or two in the afternoon, with a 2 p.m. start. Before ski school you will have collected your skis, either from the ski shop or from the storage area in your hotel or villa. It is unusual for hotels in Europe to allow skis into the main body of the hotel, although many American resorts have not the slightest objection to the skier keeping his full equipment in his room. Normally, in Europe, skis are stored in the hotel cellar, or perhaps an outbuilding. Skis are usually safe there, but light fingers often spirit away ski sticks; keep them in your room. Unless your hotel's boot store is within the body of the building, and thus heated, it is vital to keep your boots with you as well. This is not because they would be stolen, but because modern boots are usually made of plastic, and cold plastic is the most inflexible of materials. However, don't stand your ski boots on, or too near, a radiator. They could melt.

Put your boots on in the hotel (it is normal to do this in the lobby), and carry your skis to the ski school meeting point. Skis are most easily carried strapped together with special rubber straps which cost only a few pence at the ski shop. Without straps, your skis will scissor when you carry them, which is both uncomfortable and dangerous. Also for safety, it is best to carry your skis with the tips in front of you. Skis are carried balanced on one shoulder and steadied with a hand.

Traditionalists suggest you should also carry your ski sticks strapped to the skis. Personally, I prefer to use the sticks to steady myself when walking in ski boots on pavements which are often rutted with packed ice. Be very careful as you walk around carrying skis. If you see a friend on the other side of the street, and turn quickly to say hello, you could send the end of your skis through a shop window, or decapitate some harmless passer-by.

When you book into ski school, you will usually be asked what standard you are. People coming from non-ski countries—Britain, Holland, Belgium or Denmark for example—would normally answer by giving the number of times they have skied: you are a beginner, or you have skied for one, two or three years. The school will know then roughly what sort of standard you are. If there is further questioning, as there might be if you are taking private lessons, or if the school is very thorough, make sure you do not over-estimate your ability. Just because you did one parallel turn on the last afternoon of the previous year's holiday, do not claim that you are a parallel skier. If you do you will simply irritate the instructor, infuriate your fellow class members because you cannot keep up, and give yourself considerable embarrassment. If, when you get to a ski class, it emerges that you are very much better than the rest of the group, the instructor will quickly move you into a higher class. In some resorts, notably the newer French 'stations', you will see notices everywhere which give details of the standards required in each class level. Simply mark off your abilities and you will know which class is yours.

If you can afford it, learning with a private instructor for the first two or three days will save you a week of toiling in ski class. A pre-snow course on a dry ski slope, added to initial lessons on snow with a private tutor, will really accelerate your learning. Private lessons are usually moderate in price—about double the hourly rate for a London secretary. Unless you are very fit, it is unlikely that you will be able to cope with more than three hours' private tuition for the first two days. Nine hours' private tuition, shared perhaps with one friend, is worth twenty hours of ski school, except that it will be more work and fewer laughs.

You will find that there are two types of private instructor. One is the sort who is probably a full-time professional ski tutor in the winter and a mountain guide in the summer. His services will be expensive because he makes his living giving private instruction.

It is more likely that you will obtain the services of a part-time instructor—usually a student, or perhaps a farmer. These men and women normally take ski school classes but give private lessons before and after the ski school day, and during the two-hour lunch break. If I want private lessons, I normally prowl the mountain looking for an instructor whose style I like and listen while he or she gives tuition to an English-speaking class. I then approach and ask if the instructor is free to give a private lesson. Usually a fee and a meeting place are negotiated there and then. Sometimes the enquiry is diverted to the ski school, which is the official channel. If you are travelling with a tour operator, the local representative should know which instructors are the most sympathetic and which ones speak your language.

When you arrive at the ski school meeting point, particularly if this is your first time, remember that most of the people around you are also newcomers, so don't feel too nervous. The first practical thing you will have to do is put on your skis. If possible dig the heel of one of your skis into the snow along with the ski sticks, and place your other ski flat on the ground. Make sure the ski is level and will not slide away—this may sound stupid but in fact half the time you will forget. Check as far as you can that there is no snow on the ski between the bindings, and underneath your boot. Then step into your bindings. The buckle of your safety strap should be on the outside and this will help to indicate which ski is which (it is not important if you cannot tell). Do up the safety strap, steady yourself on one of your ski sticks and repeat the process with your other ski. Make sure that your skis are on firmly. Jump up and down a few times. A piece of snow or dirt can sometimes prevent a proper fit.

The basic object of every ski instructor is to give his pupils the skills to get down the mountain as smoothly and gently as possible. Style is not the goal: it is the means to an end, and that end is surely enjoyment. The better you ski, in the normal sense of perfecting your turns, the more enjoyment you will get, because you can relax more, take everything you meet in your stride, and use far less energy. The near-perfect skier who comes flowing down the *piste* is expending far less effort than the intermediate who every few yards has to think just how he is going to cope with the next problem. But such perfection is rare and if we were all broken-hearted for failing to achieve it, the slopes would run with tears.

Beginner

Most ski schools today still follow a basic teaching system which is roughly the same, whatever the length of skis used. Your first lesson will largely consist of getting used to skis. They do feel very peculiar the first time you wear them—uncomfortable, large, awkward. But without them you would sink deep into the snow and not be able to move around the mountain at all. In that first lesson your instructor will show you how to walk and climb in skis, how to fall, get up and do standing turns. All these manoeuvres will help you towards understanding your skis, showing you that they can be managed and that skiing is not the alarmingly difficult activity it might have appeared at first.

Almost certainly within the first twenty minutes the instructor will take you to the top of a little mound, point you downhill, and give you a little push. You will then find that you can actually move, that you will stop as soon as you run out of downhill slope, and that if you fall it is not terribly painful. Towards the end of the first lesson you will be learning the basic stopping procedures, and perhaps some turns. You will have to do a great deal of climbing. The instructor is not being malicious; he wants to loosen up those neglected city muscles and get you used to ski boots. At the end of the first hour you will want a beer or a coffee . . . and will have earned it.

The Terms
During lessons your ski instructor will shout various things at you, and it helps if you know roughly what he means. The words he will bandy about include:

Fall line This is the most direct line down the slope, the line a ball would take if you rolled it down the mountain. Most ski movements are planned around the fall line and you will use the pull of gravity a great deal in your later movements on skis. There are minor fall lines within the main, straight-down-the-mountain line. A gully or hillock will have its own fall line, and when you are in a gully or on a hillock you must concern yourself with that fall line. Most of the time your instructor will be saying . . . 'do this *when you come into the fall line*', which means when you are facing directly down the slope, or . . . '*keep your skis horizontal to the fall line*', and that is across the slope, e.g. parallel with the river that runs in the valley below.

Edge The edge of your ski is the metal strip that runs right round the lower outside. It is normally kept fairly sharp to give the ski some bite. When the instructor says 'edge' one or both skis, he means that you should angle your ski to dig an edge into the snow. Correct edging is the magic key of skiing. Your instructor will tell you that you are not edging enough, or perhaps edging too much. Falls, particularly at speed, are sometimes caused by 'catching an outside edge', another way of saying that the skier wrongly positioned his ski and thus presented the outside of the ski to some mound or bump in the snow.

Schuss This is a straight downhill run at speed. Instructors often end their lessons with a modest schuss to finish the day on a high note. A *schuss* is not half as dangerous as it looks. So when the instructor says '*schuss* down here', just put your skis together, point them downhill, relax, and go.

Weight Balance is important to good skiing and you will often be told to put your weight forward, backwards, or on one ski or another. Try to imagine where your weight is concentrated, your centre of gravity. When you stand erect, it is somewhere around your tummy. Lean forward, and your centre of gravity moves forward too, until you reach the point where you fall over. While you are doing this, try to keep your weight concentration low. If you bend forward too much from the waist, you push your centre of gravity up towards your shoulders and you become unstable.

When you bend from the knees your weight is concentrated more around your hips. You may be tempted to push your bottom out backwards when your shoulders go forward. This simply leaves your centre of gravity where it was but at the same time removes such flexibility of movement as you have. 'Unweighting' is lifting your weight from the skis in ways which will be discussed later.

Piste The general term in Europe for a ski run. In America the word is 'run', or 'trail' for something narrower. If your instructor says you are going to go 'off-*piste*' you will know he is taking you off the prepared runs, usually to give you wider experience of differing snow conditions. *Pistes* are normally marked in different colours. A green marker indicates a slope which is virtually a promenade and should be suitable for first-day skiers. A blue run is normally a good, wide, gentle slope where pupils can try out newly-acquired skills. A red run provides entertainment for inter-mediate-to-good skiers, often with the occasional difficulties. Black runs represent the strongest challenge on the prepared *pistes* of a particular resort. Avoid black runs unless you are a competent all-round skier. Black run obstacles frequently include very steep slopes, which are intimidating to the inexperienced, or narrow gullies over tricky terrain.

Moguls When your instructor says, 'I will take you into the moguls', do not expect to be introduced to the local aristocracy; they are in fact a series of hillocks on a *piste*. These hillocks are created by a succession of skiers turning in the same place. Once a mogul is created, it is used time and time again by other skiers as an aid to turning, and is thus accentuated in size. A modest mogul field is a pleasure to ski; a fierce one can be uncomfortable. As you progress to intermediate turns you will learn to love moguls. They are normally found over the brow of a ridge where the run becomes steeper.

Walking The first thing you will have to do on skis is to walk—and initially you will find it a very awkward process. Even with short skis you will tend to slip backwards, cross the tips, and feel

59

generally unsteady. (If you don't, you are well on the way to becoming an expert.) But that uncertainty will disappear very quickly indeed, and you will soon learn that those planks on your feet can be controlled. Once you have put on skis, it will take you about ten minutes to discover that you can walk quite normally in them. The essence of the walk is to keep the soles of the ski on the ground and just slide them along the snow. Lean forward a little and give yourself an extra push, and extra support from the ski sticks.

Deliberately dig the stick into the snow a little ahead of you. Make sure the stick tip is a couple of inches away from the side of the ski; otherwise you may run the ski over the basket and face the nuisance of not being able either to move to get the ski off the basket, or to get the ski off the basket until you can move . . . If you see what I mean.

Everyone's introduction to skiing. A dozen pupils is the norm, but if you have fewer than this in your first classes you will progress faster. Here, the instructor is showing his class that skiing on one ski is not impossible—the aim is to relax the beginner and make him more confident.

It is important that you relax. Beginners walking on skis create problems for themselves by tending to bend forward, as if bowing to some passing dignitary, rather than gently leaning forward. If you push your weight too far forward in the walk, the skis will simply start to slide backwards. If you start to slip back, stand up and put your sticks into the snow behind you to steady yourself before beginning again. Ignore the skier who comes whizzing past you while you struggle; three days ago he was probably on his first skis too.

Step-turn Having managed the walk, the next thing you will want to do is turn. This is possible on flat ground with very simple movements. Start with your skis together, then raise the tip of the ski nearest the direction you want to turn and move it a foot or so towards your destination. You must keep the heel of this ski on the ground while you are moving the tip. Bring the tip back to the ground and, still with your ski heels together, move the second ski tip to close with the first. By repeating this process you can make a star pattern in the snow, turning the full 360 degrees if you wish. Use your ski sticks throughout to steady yourself. Don't make each step of the star much more than twelve inches; you will simply unbalance yourself. There is no point in spending too much time practising this as you should very quickly outgrow it, moving on instead to the kick-turn.

Falling down and getting up Within a few minutes of getting on skis you may well have had your first fall. It is then that you discover that falling in snow is not necessarily an unpleasant or painful experience. If you feel yourself falling the best procedure is just to sit down, slightly to one side of your skis. Don't worry; your ski pants are waterproof. Most falls that you see on the slopes are 'sitting down' falls, which are the automatic reactions of skiers who find themselves out of control.

But whatever the way of your falling, there is an art to getting up again. Rule one is to relax. Don't try to scramble up and pretend nothing has happened. Look around and settle down. Try to get yourself into a sitting position with your bottom uphill, above your skis. Place your skis parallel, and across the fall line, so they won't slide away the moment you put your weight on them. Dig your stick ends into the snow beside and slightly behind you, and push yourself up onto your feet. When you do this you will discover one of the reasons for baskets: they stop the ski stick going deep into the snow. Once standing, brush yourself down, move your feet around to ensure that your boots are firmly in your bindings, decide where you want to go next, and then proceed on your way.

Kick-turn This is your first real turn and is one that will come in useful throughout your skiing life. It is a stationary turn which is far better demonstrated by an instructor than described in a book. Normally, you will use it when a moving turn is impossible, such as when you run off the *piste* into deep snow, perhaps with rocks around. In your early stages, however, you may use the kick-turn quite a lot to get yourself back on the right track. It is much favoured by ski instructors because it also makes for very healthy exercise, particularly if you are using longish skis!

To start a kick-turn you place your skis together across the fall line, so that there is no chance of their moving. Your shoulders should be squared to the mountain. You dig your ski sticks into the snow behind you, one on either side of your body and each a foot or so (the distance will depend on the length of your sticks) from the parallel skis. The downhill ski (the one furthest down the mountain) is then kicked up so that it becomes vertical. There will be a moment when your leg is in the air, parallel to the ground, and your face is opposite the tip of your ski. Then you twist the up-right ski so that it faces in the opposite direction from the grounded

Kick-turn.

ski, and put it back down on the snow. Your skis should now be as close to parallel to one another as you can make them, and less than a foot apart. Make sure you are steady, then swing the other ski and your body round so that the two skis are once again close together, and your 180-degree turn is complete. Be careful not to catch the heel of your ski on the ski stick which is supporting you as you swing round. It sounds a lot more complicated than it is. Your ski instructor will make it look infuriatingly easy. Part of the secret is to make sure that the ski sticks will support your full weight if you are temporarily unbalanced. With modern short skis the manoeuvre is very easy indeed.

Side-stepping To come down any mountain, you will first have to go up, and no self-respecting ski instructor is going to let you use a lift until you can do the basic climb, in other words the side-step. The side-step, like the kick-turn, is a basic ski essential which you will always use, whatever your standard. In essence, it is the process of making a little staircase in the snow with your skis, and then using those steps to climb the mountain.

In the side-step you walk sideways uphill, making sure all the time that your skis are across the fall line. Be careful not to let the tips or heels point up or down the mountain; if you do you will start to slide. Climb the mountain steadily, putting the uphill ski a foot or so up the mountain with each step. Keep the sole of each ski horizontal—that is, at an angle to the slope. In this way you will make those 'steps' with built up snow as the skis bite in, and discover the reason for edging. As long as your skis are across the fall line, and as long as the skis are edged, you will feel secure.

At first you will find your skis wandering about almost with a will of their own, but gradually you'll get used to handling them. You will also find that your ski sticks are very useful, although occasionally you might step on your ski stick basket. Side-stepping up and down hills is good exercise; it is also a technique you will use a great deal during your ski career. Normally you will combine your side-stepping with walking, which means that you will be making an upwards crossing of the slope.

In these early stages of learning, try to avoid deep snow. If you stray from the prepared ski area you will find yourself unable to handle your skis. It is an added burden which is pointless for the first few days of instruction. Later you will enjoy deep snow, and indeed go hunting for it to luxuriate in the excitement of sinking up to your waist in 'powder' . . . but not yet. If you do go into deep snow, particularly when it is warm or late in the season, be careful not to try too energetic an escape. You might twist an ankle or knee.

Herringbone A much quicker way of getting up hills than the side-step is the herringbone, named after the pattern which the tracks make in the snow. This is a sort of 'second gear' for uphill progress, and is used on slopes of medium steepness which are too much to walk straight up, but not steep enough to justify a side-step.

Side-stepping.

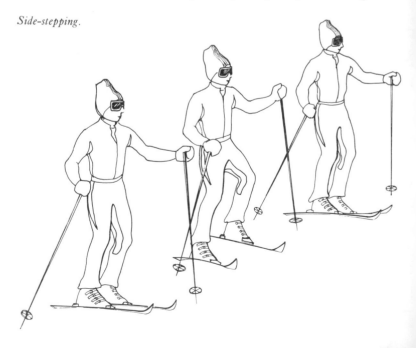

Herringbone.

Face up the hill, with your ski tips apart and the heels together. Your sticks should be behind you and your weight supported on them. Walk forward maintaining the angle of the skis and making sure that you edge the sole of the ski against the slope. If you keep your feet well apart, this edging will be automatic. For once lean into the slope, pushing yourself upward with the sticks, which are always behind you. If the mountain gets too steep for the herringbone to be practical it is easy to swing one ski across to be parallel with the other, and to start side-stepping instead.

Traverse Another key movement. Traversing is the technique of running straight across the fall line, leaving a trail which should be like the contour marks on a map. To start a traverse your instructor will first teach you how to stand on the slope. This involves edging the skis to give yourself a nice flat step. Your body should be fairly upright from a side view, with a slight bend of the knees to absorb any bumps.

From the front view (in other words, from the other side of the fall line) your body should take up the classic 'comma' stance, with shoulders slightly out from the mountain and hips in. Both hands should be low, helping you to keep a low centre of gravity. Your downhill hand should be just behind your bottom, and your uphill hand just in front of your hip. This will slightly twist your upper torso into the correct weight position. Point your knees straight. (You will find that you lead with your knees in most ski manoeuvres, and the traverse is no different.) The tip of the uphill ski should be three or four inches in front of the downhill. Keep your skis parallel and fairly close together. Almost all your weight is on the lower ski—say, sixty or seventy per cent.

Comma position.

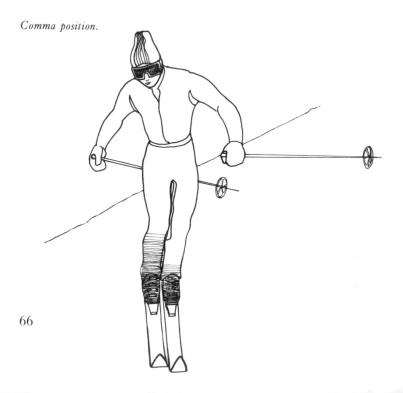

An important thing to remember in the traverse is to avoid crouching forward, which will be your first reaction. Try to keep your weight over your feet. To go straight across the mountain you will have to point your skis slightly downhill. The edging of the skis will keep you on the straight because, in fact, they will be turning you imperceptibly all the time, and thus compensating for your slight downhill steering. You will soon learn to adjust the edging or your skis to give yourself a greater turn, or to let yourself go a little further down the fall line.

Snowplough—glide and brake The first time you stand on skis, or perhaps even before that, you will look around and say: 'Well, yes, but if I move . . . how do I stop?' The snowplough is a basic braking procedure for slow speed skiing. Some ski schools do not teach it any more until fairly late in the course of lessons. The reason is that it is very easy to become addicted to the snowplough; it feels so safe. But it is also an important part of any skier's armament and should not, therefore, be overlooked. You should be doing snowploughs within the first hour of being on skis.

You will start your first snowplough from the top of a gentle slope. If you are in ski school you will have the pleasure of watching your ski companions attempt the same manoeuvre. Watch what they do; try to see what they do right and what they do wrong. When your turn comes you must imagine that you are making exactly what the word says, a snowplough. Your skis are placed with the tips together but heels far apart—'Get your legs as wide apart as is impossible,' my first instructor used to tell his class. The skis are edged in, in such a way as to make a 'plough', with the tips carving a path through the snow. The sharper the walls of the plough, the more severe the braking power. You control the angle of the skis against the snow by using your knees and ankles. When you move your knees forward and towards each other—while keeping your feet apart—the braking action is increased. If you ease the bend of your knees, you will gather a little speed. Very quickly you will find that you have quite precise control of your speed.

Absorbing the bumps.

Straight running Your instructor will normally discuss straight running before going on to the snowplough, but the preoccupation of most beginners with stopping means that perhaps the snowplough should be at least described earlier. Straight running is the technique of moving down a slight slope in a straight line. You stand at the top of the slope, having made sure that it flattens out at the bottom, and just let yourself go. Your feet should be twelve inches apart at the most and your knees slightly bent to absorb any small bumps. Keep your body as upright as possible, apart from the knees.

You can put the snowplough and straight running together, easing the braking action until you feel confident and then sliding your skis together. You will be able to revert to a snowplough quickly if you feel the need.

Snowplough turn This is your first moving turn, and with it you will be able to ski down the mountain. Once you have mastered the snowplough turn the easier slopes of the resort will be within your powers.

Gather a little speed and you will find that by shifting your weight from the middle to the uphill ski, you will turn. At first, try not to change the angle of your feet or knees; simply drop your

uphill shoulder. This will move some weight to the ski below the shoulder you have dipped. Once the weight goes on to one ski rather than the other, you will turn and the ski on which you have placed your weight will swing into the downhill position. So, dip your left shoulder and you will turn right, dip your right shoulder and you will turn left.

If you find this doesn't happen it probably means that you are subconsciously trying to compensate for the shoulder movement by sticking your bottom out. You can accentuate the weight change by bending one knee. If you slightly bend the left knee, pointing the kneecap at the tip of your left ski, you will turn right. If it still doesn't work, get your instructor to take you aside and tell you what you are doing wrong, because there is something amiss. But as a final aid you might try looking over one shoulder at the heel of the ski you wish to be at the outside of the turn. Doing this will force you to take an upright position, and dip your shoulder, and bend your knee. You surely must turn then!

Once you are going in your chosen direction, centralise your weight again and you will stop turning. Then bring your skis together gently, and put a little more weight on the downhill ski. Advance the upper ski an inch or so ahead, and you are back in the traverse position.

Snowplough turn.

Try to find wide open gentle slopes on which to practise these turns. Most villages have nursery slopes designed for this purpose but you may find that the snow is more suitable higher up the mountain. After a few practice turns you will find that you can link the turns, first left and then right, with a little traverse every now and then. Once you are doing this, you can claim to be a skier. You could go down any mountain, given reasonable snow conditions and a good width of *piste*. Practise a great deal on slopes that you can handle, however. If you rush too quickly on to the trickier stuff you will find yourself intimidated by height or steepness; this will set your confidence back.

Intermediate

Graduation day from the beginner slopes is a great day in any skier's life. You should do this on the second or third day of tuition, after about four hours of lessons. If you have been to dry ski school before your holiday, the graduation will be even sooner.

Stem-turn The stem-turn is a natural development of the snowplough. It is not a difficult transition, providing you have full control of your snowploughs. The stem, which is simply a half snowplough, gives you greater flexibility than the snowplough itself, which is also known as the double stem.

From the traverse position the skier 'stems', that is eases out, his uphill ski. The weight is then transferred to that uphill ski in the same way that it was in the snowplough and, as with the snowplough, so the turn will be completed. Do everything gently, bending the knee on which your weight is being placed. Just before you enter the turn, your shoulders will be in the traverse position, facing slightly downhill. Now swing your shoulders to face very slightly uphill. You are thus *counter-rotating*, which is a description you will hear later in your ski career. Counter-rotation is twisting the upper body in the opposite direction to the way in which you intend to turn. It moves your body weight into the correct position and makes the turn easier. It is like tightening the spring of a clock.

Stem-turn.

If you have difficulty in completing a stem turn it is usually because you forget to bend your upper knee when you stem the uphill ski. This means that your weight is still on the lower ski. Keep the knee bent throughout the turn. You will be tempted to straighten again when you reach the fall line—that is, when you are pointing directly downhill. If you unbend then you will carry on going straight down the slope, and early intermediates tend to get alarmed at that stage and sit down. Keep your knee bent until you are actually pointing in the direction you wish to be, then centralise your weight and come back to the traverse.

The stem turn needs a great deal of practice. The essence of the turn is to do things smoothly and with thought; it will come naturally later. You may find that, as you move your weight to the upper ski, the lower one, freed of its burden, tries to wander off. Try to maintain control over the direction of that lower ski, without actually applying very much weight. In particular see that the tips of both skis neither wander too far apart, nor cross. If you act too hastily in the stem turn, the two skis tend to carry on in different directions, because the lower ski is still edged for the traverse, while the upper ski is turning. If you make sure that there is not too much edge on that lower ski, your turn will be smooth. As you stem, do so without lifting the ski from the ground . . . slide it out slowly. Bend those knees, both of them, but the upper knee a little more than the lower.

Having succeeded with the stem turn you will be among the mass of skiers who are enjoying their holidays rather than working at it. Most of the runs in an average resort will be open to you and, in the bar at the end of the ski-day, you will be swopping stories with the best of them. Do not be too concerned at this stage if you find your success varies. You will ski better one day than the next. This is usually the product of different snow conditions, or perhaps because you have worked so hard on Monday that by Tuesday those newly-taxed muscles are a little tired.

Side-slipping This is another weapon in your armoury. It will get you out of tricky situations and provide some of the most exhilarating ski experiences. Side-slipping looks, and indeed is, a simple technique. But it is more than that. The side-slip needs confidence and control of the skis in parallel. Master the side-slip and you have taken a really major step towards becoming a complete skier.

To side-slip you must release the edges which are holding you steady on the mountain. The gradual release of the edge will let you slip down the slope. The more you release, the faster you will go. To stop, you simply edge fully once more. Your instructor will show you how to do this standing still, but sometimes the skis need a little encouragement to slip when you start from a stationary

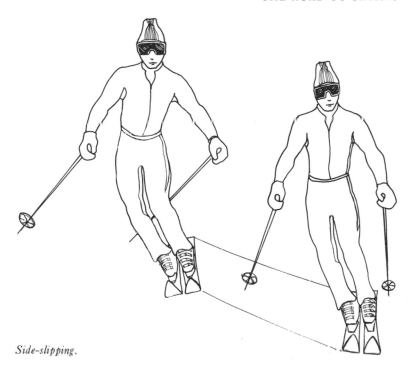

Side-slipping.

position. It is much simpler from a moving traverse, which is when you will use the side-slip most of the time anyway. Start traversing across the slope and then release the edges of your skis. Do so gently. If you completely flatten your skis against the slope you run the risk of catching the outside edge against some lump or bump and toppling over. Once you have slipped a foot or so, return to the normal traverse position. Then try again. With practice at traversing, releasing and traversing again, you will learn to make controlled progress across a slope. It will help you to choose the point where you are going to turn, to wend your way through the moguls, and to become an all-round skier.

The key to successful side-slipping is the position of the knees. As we have seen already, and will see again, you can steer yourself with the position of your knees. Skis tend always to follow the direction in which your knees are pointing. In the side-slip, if you move your knees out slightly from the mountain, you will side-slip down and forwards; if you move your knees towards the mountain, you will come back into a controlled traverse again. But keep your knees bent, otherwise you will not be able to point your direction with them.

You can side-slip straight down the fall line, backwards (by leaning your weight over the heel of your skis) or forwards. It is a simple but not always easy manoeuvre, particularly in less than perfect snow conditions. So do not worry too much if it takes a little time to get it right. Practice, practice, practice is the answer. Fortunately, the forward side-slip is a fun move to practice.

Hockey stop You can halt any forward progress very rapidly indeed with a hockey stop and, having learnt the traverse and the side-slip, the hockey stop will give you no problems. This turning action takes its name from the quick, neat stop which skaters employ in ice hockey. Take as sharp a descent line down the mountain as you feel your nerves will stand and, when you have gathered enough speed to feel that you have the ability to move the skis around on

Hockey stop.

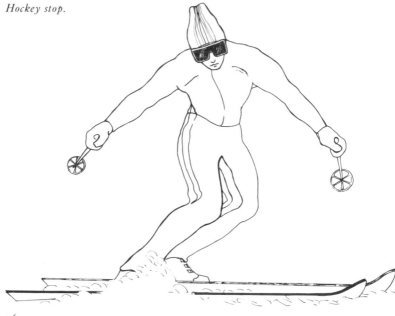

the snow, go into the hockey stop.

Lower yourself nearer the ground by bending at the hip and knees. Steer your knees in the direction you wish to go across the fall line and drive your skis out across it. As you turn, bring your weight down hard on the skis, using your bent legs to force the skis away from you. You will stop. It is the hockey stop that you will rely on most of all in your future skiing. As you gain confidence you will increase the angle from which you start the hockey stop.

Uphill christie The uphill christie is not quite as sharp as the hockey stop, and much more of a turn. The christies are a whole family of ski turns which originated in Christiania, the one time name for Oslo. This is the first of the real parallel turns. Start in the traverse and then point your skis slightly downhill. As you gather speed move the lower half of your legs forward and turn your knees slightly towards the slope. This action will edge your skis and you will start to turn. As you complete the turn and the ski tips start to face uphill, straighten up a little; the force of your legs against the skis will bring you to a halt.

Unweighting—up and down As you move on to the next set of turns, your instructor will start to talk about 'unweighting'. By unweighting you are temporarily reducing the load on your skis, normally to start a turn. The theory of unweighting is straight-forward enough. Experiment at home. Stand on the floor with your knees slightly bent, then straighten up fairly rapidly. Your feet might even leave the ground with the force of your rise. Similarly if you take up the same standing position, and then suddenly bend your knees even more, the weight on your feet is greatly reduced. The first of these movements is upwards unweighting, and the second, downwards unweighting.

On skis these simple movements need a great deal of practice because unweighting has to be timed properly. It is no use, for example, to unweight, have a little ponder, and then try to turn. When you actually come to make the manoeuvre your full weight will be back on the skis again.

Frequently the ski terrain will give you natural assistance for unweighting. A small bump on the *piste* will make you bend your knees and then, as you reach the top, your skis will float away as they have the weight of your body temporarily removed. You can use this natural unweighting to make turns. The use of these bumps for such turning is very popular with skiers of all standards, which is why moguls grow. The constant flow of skiers choosing the same place to turn gradually carves a bigger and bigger mogul.

You will find that there is a considerable enthusiasm at the moment in many resorts, notably in Austria, for down unweighting in the early stages of turn initiation. Down unweighting is more difficult to learn than up unweighting, and extremely difficult to switch to if you have been educated in the hop-hop-hop style of the 'sixties. But if learnt from the earliest stage, down unweighting is a much more effective way of skiing in the long term, particularly if you wish to become a fast skier. Up unweighting temporarily places you in a position of delicate balance, and you can find your-

Down unweighting.

78

self thrown by a sudden unseen bumpiness in the terrain as you are making a turn.

If your ski instructor insists on down unweighting, it makes little difference to the turns described in these pages, except that instead of raising yourself immediately before the turn you should compress sharply—bending your knees even further than usual—in order to remove the weight from your skis. At the moment of unweighting you initiate the turn.

If you have been taught to up unweight try to find an instructor who is not going to bully you into changing. Unless you intend to be a slalom racer, up unweighting will serve you well—and it looks more graceful anyway.

Stem christie This is the work-horse turn of modern skiing. Experts and purists try to resist that fact, but most skiers use the stem christie as their basic turn. It may be a pity, but well-executed stem christies are often as far as the recreational skier goes in his ski education. There is no real harm in this, except that the stem skier is robbed of the magic world of parallel skiing. With the stem christie, and a measure of confidence, you will be able to descend very testing runs.

It is worth remembering before you start learning the stem christie that it is a manoeuvre which you will acquire gradually. At first, it is likely that your stem turns will persist, and that you will be psychologically unwilling to make the more dramatic movements required by the christie. Don't worry. Each turn will see a slight improvement.

To begin the stem christie, you will need to be travelling at a reasonable but not excessive speed. Stem the uphill ski, as if you are about to do a stem turn, and lower your weight at the same time by bending your knees (beware: do not bend forward from the waist). Up unweight by straightening your knees, keeping such pressure as remains on the uphill ski. The skis will fall into the fall line. Because the inside ski has almost no weight on it, it should slide of its own accord into parallel with the outer ski. But give it any assistance you feel necessary.

The bringing together of the skis is an alarming moment the

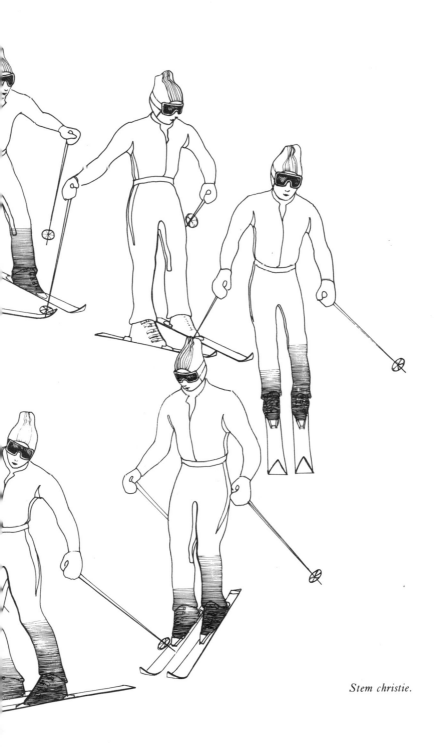

Stem christie.

first time you experience it. There you are, with your skis together pointing straight down the mountain. All you have to do then is to complete the turn with the uphill christie, with your skis together and, using your weight, edging the skis round until you are facing the way you want to. Simple, really.

When you first try this, two major problems are likely to arise. You will probably take fright as you reach the fall line, moving your weight from the outside ski to the central position, and perhaps leaning back. This could send you rocketing down the mountain, but it's much more likely that you'll sit down, because of your apprehension. Instead, keep a grip on the turn, with shoulders slightly squared to the outside of the circle you are making—that is, with the back of your head to the mountain—and you will get round safely. Obviously you will accelerate slightly as your weight points downhill but this is only a temporary situation.

The second problem is that you might be so relieved at having completed the turn that you will suddenly switch your weight and turn to face the mountain. This will simply swing you round sharply, and your ski heels will point down the mountain. So take care to keep your weight on the downhill ski and your shoulders squared to the mountain. At first, as you practise these turns, you should find a wide *piste* which will give you plenty of time to recover and get back into the traverse position. Try to get well settled into the traverse before you stop. It is a bad habit to turn, and then stop to get yourself together. That way you will never get into the flow of skiing, which is the core of the sport's real pleasure. Assemble yourself . . . feel that you could make another turn if you chose to, and then stop if you want to.

Try to learn your stem christies early in a ski-week, and you will move on to full parallels before the end of the week. Otherwise you run a great risk of becoming addicted to stemming.

In the stem christie, some ski instructors may insist that you stem the downhill ski, moving your weight up to the other ski as you do so. The idea of teaching this way is to prevent the habit of stemming becoming too cemented in the skier's mind. There is very little difference in the end product and the 'stem the downhill ski' school of thought is a very small one. Don't get cross if your instructor insists upon it; at least it shows that he has given some thought to easing your present rate of learning, and is concerned about your future programmes.

Importance of the sticks So far your ski sticks have seemed less a vital part of skiing than an aid when you have been in trouble. In the early moves, so much accent is placed on weighting, unweighting, and edging that to discuss ski sticks would be to over-complicate the issue. However, as you come to the christie family of turns the importance of your sticks will become rapidly apparent. You will, in fact, use your sticks as a crucial part of the turns. The flow of your upper body, encouraged by the placing of the sticks, will ease your way smoothly down the slope.

In the stem christie, as in other turns, try to ground the ski stick at the point where you intend to turn, and then turn around it as if it were a marking point. Do not thrust the stick too far ahead of you; placing it a couple of feet in front of your toe will force your downhill shoulder forward into the correct position. As you reach your ski stick, so your body will be raised automatically (and thus you are up unweighting). Make sure you remove your stick the moment you reach the fall line; otherwise it will pull you round so that your shoulders are facing the wrong way again.

The flow of skiing As you grow confident in your turns, and are able to switch from traverse to turn, to side-slip, to hockey stop, as you feel your growing ability to handle different types of problems, so you will discover the flow of skiing. The variations of the mountain terrain which were so worrying when you first started will become the source of a great deal of pleasure. You will find that you can link the turns and proceed down the mountain as if you yourself were a stream, finding the best way down the slopes, without hesitation and without rest; as you perfect your turns, they will become increasingly effortless.

Advanced

Moving from intermediate skiing to advanced parallel skiing is a major step, and one which many skiers never manage to achieve. There are serious practical and psychological barriers between the two styles. The psychological problem is that intermediate stem skiing is adequate for almost every type of terrain. With fairly modest adaptation, it will take you through the deepest snow on the steepest slope. The objection is that it is a bit ragged, and is not really suitable for higher speeds. The skier therefore has to be convinced that there is a need to progress to a higher level of skiing efficiency. By the time he is convinced, he may have been a stem skier for several years, having reached basic christie level in one or two seasons and then given up lessons.

You will either love them, or hate them. Moguls are small hills carved from the snow as a result of skiers constantly turning at the same point. You can turn on the tops of each bump, or carve your way through the little valleys.

To cope with this, in Britain at least, there are summer dry slope conversion courses aimed at taking skiers who have never done anything else but stem christies, and upgrading them to parallel turns. It usually takes six to eight hours to break the habit and the courses are often fully booked; the urge for self-improvement is everywhere.

The practical problem of conversion to parallel skiing is that the skier may be using equipment which is too old. If you bought skis when you first started the sport, they may be 'tired'—and almost certainly the edges will need sharpening. Have your ski shop check your equipment before the season starts. Check your boots, too. If they are leather they may have too much flexibility in them for modern turns.

For learning parallel skiing you will also need to be a little fitter than for the earlier turns, although once you have acquired a parallel technique the effort required is less than that for stem christies and considerably less than for snowploughs. If you are about to go on holiday and are determined to shake the stem habit, put your heart and muscles into pre-ski exercises for at least a month or so before your departure. Your reactions will have to be prompt and coordinated.

You may also find that you want to know a great deal more about the techniques and theory behind advanced skiing than are dealt with in this book. Other works are recommended later.

Parallel christie The difference between the parallel christie and the stem christie is in the start of the turn. You will not be steering your skis in the normal way, but swinging them, and taking your weight off the skis to facilitate the start of those turns.

You start the parallel with a normal traverse. Pick out the point where you intend to turn and, as you approach this point, lower your weight slightly by bending your knees just a little more. As you plant the downhill stick into the snow a little ahead of your downhill foot you will bounce back from that initial knee bend. This upward unweighting will make your legs almost straight, and take the pressure off your skis. Steer your skis around the corner with your hips and knees, remembering that your skis will always point the way your knees are pointing. As you come into the fall line, your weight will come down again. Having removed the ski pole from the snow, you swing into the christie finish that you have been doing since your earliest days on skis.

Although all the movements are rapid, and blurred together in one continuous pattern, none of them are abrupt. Do not jump in the air, and do not thump down again at the end of the turn. Ease into it, keeping in your mind all the time that your knees are doing the steering and your shoulders keeping you upright by distributing your weight properly. Imagine that your kneecaps are, in effect, your front wheels; point them in the right path and the rest of your body will follow.

A ski instructor, particularly in France, may make you attempt fairly aggressive unweighting, to the extent of jumping before the turn. You will hear the cry, 'hop, hop, hop . . .' all the way down the slopes. This action, the *'ruade'*, was once a favoured ski technique. It was used to overcome the natural reluctance of skiers to actually take their weight off the ground. Once you have defeated this worry you can relax back into a more gentle turn.

At the start, the most difficult part of advancing to the parallel christie is losing the stem habit. The only way to overcome this is by practice under observation. It does, however, help to find some gentle bumps which will give you confidence in the unweighting and leave you more time to think about resisting the stemming. The other asset you need is speed. The faster you can go, within reason, the more willing your skis will be to turn.

Aids to the parallel When attempting the parallel turn, you have one big problem; you make so great an effort to stop the uphill ski stemming that the lower ski slips away almost unnoticed. This can be caused by the skier putting too much weight backwards on to the heel of the skis. As you approach the turn, try leaning your knees forward until you can feel the front of your boot pressing against the lower shin. Keep in that position on the early parts of the turn and you will find it much easier to keep your skis in line.

There are a variety of ways of reaching the top of your ski slope.

In all this, remember that parallel does not necessarily mean the skis are cheek to cheek. Just because there is an inch or two of space between your skis it does not mean that you are not skiing parallel. Jean-Claude Killy has shown quite clearly that an experienced and accomplished man can ski with his feet a long way apart and still be the world's best. The closer you get your skis together, the prettier you will look, but it doesn't automatically mean that you are skiing any better. You can open a four-inch gap between the skis before you feel any serious interference with your skiing. It is always possible, too, that you are a little knock-kneed, and if you press your knees together your feet will still be apart.

As you concentrate fiercely on the turn, do not worry so much that you actually look at the ski tips; this can only push your weight in the wrong direction. Always look where you are going, or down the mountain; never at your feet or behind you. This means that, in the turn, you will be looking well round and that at some point your head may be at a 90-degree angle to your skis. Similarly, over-concentration can make you 'set' in a particular stance throughout the turn. You must be flexible and adjust your position as you go round.

It is also important to practise your turns in both directions. Many skiers find it much easier to turn in one direction than the other. I certainly do. Towards the end of the day I find myself choosing to do my sharp turns to the left and then seeking a nice gentle way to turn right. It is a terrible habit. Try and prevent it by forcing yourself to do first one, then the other.

Short swing Now that you have managed a few turns with your skis parallel, you will want to move on to some of the more elegant ski techniques. High on the list of these are the short swing and the *wedeln*. There are minor differences between the two, but both produce that nice rhythmical descent which typifies the better skier. The short swing is the perfect technique for handling mogul

Private tuition is a quick, if sometimes costly, way of improving your ski technique. Here, against the spectacular backdrop of the Matterhorn, a Swiss teacher is helping his pupil.

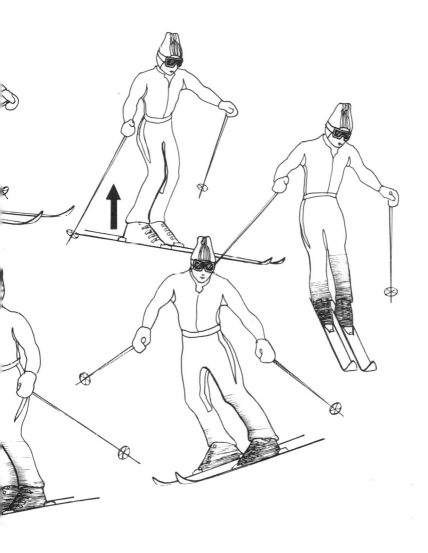

Parallel turn.

slopes, as it retains the possibility of braking within the turn without complete loss of rhythm.

Short swings are simply a series of linked christies in which you never actually enter the traverse; your line is almost straight down and you only adjust the angle of the turn to the steepness of the slope. Your upper body should remain facing down the fall line almost all the time, with only the slightest hint of counter-rotation (turning your torso in the opposite direction of the turn). The skiing is done with your legs, with very rapid re-edging of the skis as you move the turn from one direction to another. This edging will allow you to brake with your heels if your speed is getting a little out of control.

The short swing is best learnt with practice. Try to find someone who is good at it and follow him or her down. Try, however, to find someone who is not going to show off, and go zooming down the mountain without giving you a chance to see what he is doing.

To get the short swing right, you must build up a rhythm, so it is pointless to try it where you have no room for a few mistakes before you start to feel the flow. You'll need some steepness, but nothing drastic. Slowly increase the angle of the fall. By the time you have really practised you will be able to go down an almost sheer face of snow in comfort and confidence!

Wedeln (pronounced 'veydeln') *Wedeln*, which in German means the wagging of a fox's tail, is easily the most attractive style of skiing. It is similar to the short swing but much, much smoother. It takes considerable practice and some resorts offer week-long *wedeln* courses which are open to parallel skiers. Once you have perfected the *wedeln* you will be up there with the true experts. You will not be able to *wedeln* unless you have excellent coordination and therefore you should not attempt it seriously until you are confident about your overall skiing—you will only be disappointed.

The reason for this is that, in the true *wedeln*, the edge changes are very slight indeed; the more imperceptible the better. The stick movement is much less aggressive than in christie turns; you are simply using the stick as a balance aid. You will see *wedeln* skiers tapping their way down the slope with the stick points just brushing the snow occasionally, but never digging in. Again it is the knees which do the steering, but with elegance and purity. The movement comes from the hips and thighs. When you first try it, you may over-stress the lack of edging and catch an outside edge. Because the *wedeln* is done fairly quickly, these falls are likely to be forward and fast—not the most comfortable.

Learn the short swing first and then, preferably with expert tuition, make the transition to the *wedeln* tail wag. The key of the *wedeln* is to do everything with the upper leg, and to treat the snow beneath you as if it were star-dust. Be very gentle with it, so as not to bruise it. The moment you feel pressure beneath your skis, ease them up to ride the bump. Try to float, keeping your shoulders as square to the fall line as possible. The best place to practise is on a gentle slope, after you have entered it from a much steeper part of the *piste*. You can build up speed and preliminary rhythm with short swings, and then progress to the *wedeln* when the angle of the slope is enough simply to maintain your speed and not accelerate you as you loosen off your edging. Once more, do not be over-concerned about the skis being close together. A few inches of space is no worry.

Jet-turn The jet-turn is so called because of the way in which the legs 'jet' out as they are unweighted. It is an extremely fast, exciting turn for someone who prefers to go over the bumps rather than short swing through them.

To do the jet-turn, and even more to use '*avalement*', which is the next stage, you will need strong thigh and stomach muscles. If you are skiing to a standard where you are contemplating jet-turns you almost certainly must be pretty fit, but a little extra work to toughen those thighs would not come amiss.

You will normally attempt a jet turn at reasonably high speed and directly down the fall line. Your stance will be fairly upright with weight a little forward, but knees bent, as you approach a chosen mogul. Turn your shoulders in the direction in which you will eventually go. As the ground rises the top half of the body remains stable, the bump being absorbed by your knees and hips and thus bending them up sharply. As the top of the bump is reached the lower legs shoot forward—that is, jet—with considerable speed as they are completely unweighted. They usually leave the ground completely at the tips. You then use your upper body to pull the skis round, coming down to earth again with knees bent. The earlier twisting out of the body will help to 'spring' them back. At no stage in the turn is there any attempt to slow down. Indeed, as the skis begin to jet it is normal to give them a little forward shove to get things moving even quicker.

Avalement French for 'swallowing', *avalement* is just that. You keep your upper body in one plane, but your lower body absorbs all changes in the terrain. You ride the snow with skis in constant contact with the ground, and swallow the bumps as they come along. Turning on a mogul with *avalement* means absorbing the rising ground, and smoothly carving a turn down the other side by extending the legs and preparing for the next turn. *Avalement* is an almost natural development which the advanced skier will find for himself. However, so stylised did skiing become in the 'fifties and 'sixties that natural actions, like *avalement*, have to be retaught.

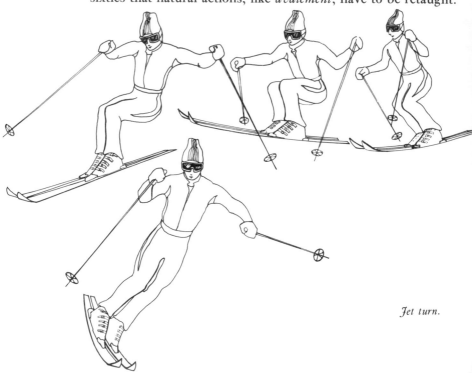

Jet turn.

The short way to skiing

There was a time when skiing took a very long time to learn, and when the beginner often gave up in disgust because most of the things that the ski instructor told him to do seemed impossible. Skis are designed to carry you over the snow, but to the sporty type that carrying had to be at the fastest possible speed. For years the accent of the business was very much on racing, so the fashion for long skis really took a grip. With these skis, beginners and intermediates feel extremely clumsy, and find it very difficult indeed to complete the simplest manoeuvres. Long skis are essential if you are to maintain your balance at high speeds; shorter equipment will refuse to hold a straight line. But in the early stages such long skis are only a hindrance.

In retrospect, it seems that the development of the short ski method of teaching was inevitable. The brain behind its development has been Cliff Taylor, a burly American with a shock of grey hair, who started his experiments with short skis in the Rockies. He developed what is now known as GLM, the Graduated Length Method. GLM usually employs four different lengths of ski. You will start on very short 100cm skis, and progress to longer ones as your ability and confidence increase. In Europe the system was quickly taken up by Robert Blanc, a Frenchman with enormous *joie de vivre* which he easily transmits to his pupils. The home of GLM in Europe, where it is called *ski évolutif*, is Les Arcs, a new station in the French Alps very close to Val d'Isère. But the method has now spread to many countries.

The GLM system has been around for some time; it is no passing fad. Now firmly established as a successful way of teaching people the basics of skiing quickly and instilling confidence, it has two major advantages over traditional methods. The fall-out rate from ski school is much lower in GLM than it is in traditional lessons, and the accident rate is also much reduced. One argument against a full GLM system is that in the long term, that is over a full ski course, it does not necessarily save time. Additionally, it involves more work and more stock for the local ski shop owner.

In your resort you will find three basic courses of short ski tuition. Pure GLM takes you quickly into parallel skiing without even bothering with snowploughs or any stem turns; GLM combination uses lengthening skis, but employs the old traditional turn techniques; and short ski traditional (which is what you will find in most of the better European ski resorts today) uses shorter skis, but not short skis, and the length does not change throughout the basic course. In the last system, the length of the skis will probably be 150cm or 165cm, although there will be local variations. You need only worry if the skis are patently giant-sized.

GLM method lessons begin by getting you used to the skis; they do not focus much on style or technique (at least this is how it will seem to the pupil). The class does limbering up exercises, little dances, and learns one or two tricks. All this teaches the skier balance, plus foot, knee and hip twisting. The first few lessons on the very shortest of skies are often without ski sticks at all. But sticks are used sparingly even in the first few lessons of traditional ski teaching, so to dispense with them altogether does not slow down progress. The skiers will be taught to come down the mountain within a few hours of trying their skis on for the first time, sometimes using the broad stance technique, but often immediately employing a fairly close parallel style of skiing. In Europe, short skis tend to be specially made with more width than in the States. There are arguments over the respective benefits of wide or narrow skis but, for the pupil, the differences are slight and the argument is strictly for the academics.

My conversion to short ski tuition came in Les Arcs a few seasons ago when I was following one of Robert Blanc's ski classes down the mountain. It was their third day of lessons. While I struggled with my medium-long skis to keep a slow speed behind them on a narrow trail, they all neatly paralleled down the hill, seemingly unaware that there were such turns as snowploughs and stem christies. Since then I have seen the GLM ski schools of America, notably the splendid ones of Steamboat Springs and Aspen, and become fully convinced of their value.

Your GLM ski teaching programme will go something like this:

Day one Having been taught how to put on your skis and walk, you will be shown straight running. After that there will be a few 'dancing' exercises, and a demonstration of 'skating' from the walk. You *may* be taught the snowplough, but you will certainly be shown some form of turn, normally using a broad stance and keeping your arms outstretched to maintain balance. In the afternoon you will probably take your first ride on a ski lift—a fairly short one. You will then come down using linked broad turns, one after another. From the distance, the ski class will look like a snake coming down the mountain.

Day two You repeat the work of the previous day's lessons, then move on to the basic elements of parallel skiing. You will be taught the uphill christie and turns from the fall line. You will learn to traverse, and by the afternoon may have graduated to the level of being given ski sticks for the first time. You will probably be doing broad turns from the traverse.

Day three By this time the men will be on 165cm skis and the women on 150cm ones. You will again go through the earlier lessons to prove that your feats on the shorter skis can also be done on longer ones. Now you will be required to do true parallel turns. First of all these will be from the fall line, which means that you will stand still facing directly down the mountain and then complete only the second half of the turn. But then they will be from the traverse, with full but very broad turns on a relatively gentle slope.

After that you will enter the same area of tuition as the traditional methods suggest. By the end of a full week, you should be well up to intermediate standards and require only practice to advance you in the expert class. (It is this practice that the beginner skier lacks and it is best to go for at least two weeks when you take your first lessons. Otherwise you risk getting stuck at the mid-intermediate stage.)

Doing your own thing

In recent years some of the stuffiness has gone out of skiing; increasingly, the whole aim of the sport has been to give pleasure and enjoyment rather than to build the ski racers of the future. In fact, as time has shown, giving pleasure and enjoyment *is* the way in which to build the ski racers of the future. This new trend means that there is much less concern about how you get down the mountain. But it also means that entire new off-beat areas of the sport are opening up. In America especially, there has been a rapid development of freestyling and hot-dogging—fun-skiing taken close to the ultimate. Freestyling is intermediate hot-dogging, when all the old rules are pushed off the cliff and you do your own thing. Inevitably there are only so many things you *can* achieve, so a whole new glossary of terms has evolved. Freestyle skiing is something everyone should try. It will give you confidence for normal skiing and teach you how to handle your skis. But give yourself plenty of room. Try these two manoeuvres for a start.

Back-flop Find a gentle straight slope on which your speed will not change dramatically. Go into a *schuss*, with your skis closely together. Flop backwards, first sitting on your skis with your bottom behind the bindings, and then completely flat on the ground with your shoulders behind the ski tails on the snow. You are, of course, still moving. When you have had enough . . . stand up. The last part is the toughest, but it is not as difficult as it sounds. This is a neat and fairly simple trick to impress the boys or girls at the ski lift as you arrive to take your place in the line.

Royal christie Once again, find a gentle slope to try this turn, which is one of the oldest in the business, but still one of the most impressive. When you do it you will sail around your turn on one leg, with the other gracefully behind you, off the ground. As you come into the turn put your weight well over the downhill ski, and slowly tip your uphill ski upwards and backwards until it is behind your back. Then, as you edge your remaining ski into the turn, move the lifted ski until it is horizontal to the ground, across your back, and held about waist high. Hold your arms out forward and sideways to give yourself extra balance. The edging will make you complete the turn and, as you come into the traverse, you can bring your raised leg down again into parallel with the other. Once you can do that, try one royal christie in each direction as the start of a series of linked turns.

Other stunts you will see, but which I don't recommend without expert help, are:

Tip roll From the traverse the skier puts both sticks firmly into the snow. He uses the sticks to raise himself onto his ski tips and swings round to land facing the same direction—a complete circle.

Window frame The difference between the window frame and the tip roll is that in the window frame technique, the skier goes forward through his planted sticks, then twists round and comes down facing back the way he came—a half circle.

Shoulder roll A forward head roll on skis.

Back scratcher From a jump the skier momentarily points his skis directly at the ground, touching his back with the tails of those skis. A nasty one if you get the timing wrong!

Spread eagle Again from a jump. The legs and arms are spread wide. The longer you can hold the position, the better it looks.

Daffy One of the most popular movements in hot-dogging. From the jump the skier puts one leg forward, keeping the ski tip directly up in the air, and the other backwards, with the tip pointing towards the ground. He then brings the skis back together before hitting the ground. A double daffy involves reversing skis in mid-air—first right ski forward, and then left.

Iron cross Another jump stunt, with the skis crossed in mid-air behind the skier's back before he lands.

Side-kick and *Fergie* The side-kick is what it says, with skis both kicked to one side after a jump. At its simplest it should be with skis held parallel, but it can be with crossed skis. The Fergie involves side-kicks to both sides before the skier lands.

Somersault A ski somersault is done in mid-air from the jump. Advanced ski hot-doggers will combine the somersault with other manoeuvres—perhaps an iron cross in the middle.

These are the basics of hot-dog competitions where the real champions get up to extraordinary tricks. One or two ski resorts now have hot-dog runs with small jumps constructed so that visitors can practise. The words 'hot dog' derive from a piece of 'forties and 'fifties colloquialism; it was the cry of admiration when someone did something spectacular.

Snow conditions

One of the fascinating aspects of snow is that it is never the same. It will vary in texture from hour to hour, in depth from yard to yard and in quality from day to day. Come down a long run in some resorts and you will ski in ideal snow at the top, with a light feathering of powder on a compacted *piste*, move on to softer granulated stuff, which will test the precision of your turns, and end up, as you approach the village shadows, in icy patches on the very bottom stretches.

Powder Off-*piste* powder skiing is surely the most dreamlike experience of the skier's repertoire. True powder is dry and made up of very small flakes. It is almost like talcum powder in its consistency. You will normally find powder very high up on the slopes and after a good fall of snow. In the right conditions—a gentle drying wind and consistently low temperatures—the powder will remain for days. Prime areas of powder are the Rockies of Colorado and Utah, some parts of the Japanese main island of Honshu and, from time to time, the alpine junction of Austria, Switzerland and Italy. True powder is rare, because it requires precipitation, that is snow, in a general atmosphere of very dry air. Usually this calls for a large landmass around the mountains. If the prevailing winds are coming from the sea it is unlikely that powder will result.

The inexperienced skier must realise the difference between powder as most resorts describe it, and powder as many of the ski books, including this one, suggest it should be. True dry powder is not a difficult thing to ski, even for a skier who has had only a few lessons. You will find true powder but rarely; when you do you will long to find it again.

The key to skiing powder is to keep your weight equally distributed on both skis. As long as you are aware of the principles of unweighting you will be all right. Falling in powder snow is not an uncomfortable experience, even if you do struggle to get up again.

The intermediate making his first few attempts at powder skiing can have trouble because someone of that standard often relies heavily on stem christies. The weight shifting involved in a stem christie makes it a tricky turn in deep snow. If you are not skiing parallel you would do better to revert to stem turns, but completing the turn with your weight evenly distributed and relying on your edges to take you around. Deep snow makes turns difficult to initiate, and equally difficult to stop. Once you take a line, the snow will try to keep you to it, so you will have to coax your way into the path you choose, rather than the one which the snow tries to choose for you.

When you venture into powder for the first time, take a long traverse. Instead of keeping your weight heavily on the lower ski, almost equalise it. If you do not, the upper ski will tend to ride up and your legs will be forced apart. If you need to gain confidence, or are forced into deep snow when you did not expect it, traverse, kick-turn, traverse, and you will get through it. Having gained confidence in the traverse, try a steeper run, almost a *schuss*. You will find that the resistance of powder means that you will not have that alarming acceleration that you find on a prepared *piste*. If you are going into a dip and then up a slight hill on the other side, advance one ski twelve inches or so ahead of the other. This has the effect of lengthening your total contact on the snow and rides you through the dip without any risk of the ski tip digging itself in.

If you ski parallel, your absorbing technique and *avalement* will come into its own. Both skis must act together. Do not unweight too sharply; although up unweighting can accentuate the floating feeling, most good skiers prefer down unweighting in deep snow. It helps if you imagine that you are on water skis, and that you are riding the waves. In most deep snow situations you will have plenty of room, so make your first turns very broad, once again as if you were sweeping round behind a speedboat. If you fix that thought in your mind it may help you to keep your tips up, put your weight a little back, and bank into your turns.

You will be tempted to sit too far back in the deep powder, particularly when you watch powder experts, as they will seem almost to be sitting down. In fact if you do sit right back, you will give yourself too much tail resistance and it will be difficult to make turns. By all means get the weight further back than during on-*piste* skiing, but please don't overdo it. The appearance of sitting down comes because you are skiing at speed and therefore probably using *avalement*.

When you have a little experience in deep snow you will be able to go almost directly down the fall line, making those exhilarating continuous trails in the snow. Ideally you will do this with a mixed *wedeln* technique using *avalement*; but you may have more fun, and certainly use more energy, if you fight the slope with aggressive counter-rotation of the shoulders. This will work very well in extremely deep, very powdery conditions—the sort of snow the average skier finds once in a hundred ski days, if he is very lucky.

Crud More politely known in Europe as crust or harsch, crud is what it sounds. Thoroughly nasty. It is the snow you find in warmer weather and towards the end of the season. There is a firmish top layer of snow through which you break from time to time to more snow of indeterminate depth underneath. The very nature of crud makes it difficult to ski, partly because the skier is nervous about it. The only sure and assertive way of dealing with crud is to kick it around. Make sure that your edges are firm and quickly made, and that there is nothing ragged about your weight movements. Use your sticks aggressively. Unless you are confident enough to do all this . . . slow down, and admit you are in something you are not quite able to handle. Then you change tactics and treat the snow gently. There are two types of snow which are traps for the unwary skier and potentially leg-breaking. One is crud, and the other is corn snow.

Corn Snow (or sugar snow) This snow is so named because each granule looks like a sweet corn seed. It is caused by continual thawing and re-freezing of old snow, and you will quite frequently find corn snow if you go glacier skiing in the summer. Corn snow can give rewarding skiing while it is cold. It will give you little trouble and it is surprisingly easy to stop on it. When corn snow warms, however, it becomes murderous. It is very sticky and often dotted with areas of true slush, which is neither snow nor water. The theory of slush skiing is that a fairly straight line down the mountain is acceptable since the tails of your skis will control your speed as you do linked turns. In practice it takes courage to ski slush and if you can avoid it, do. You'll have more fun and security at the bottom of the mountain drinking glühwein.

Ice Various factors will produce ice, but you will usually encounter it at the end of a run where there has been a large traffic of skiers and the *piste* has been polished. It is essential that your skis are suitable if you are going to encounter a great deal of ice. This means particularly that your ski edges should be sharp, so that you can grip the ice firmly.

Semi-ice, which is well-polished snow, is quite skiable and can be pleasant in small bursts. Real ice, the pale blue stuff which can form when a stream has spilt over the *piste*, is unskiable. If there is a lot of real ice about, give up; you could do yourself a great deal of damage. From now on, the word 'ice' means polished hard snow.

You should go into ice turns in an attacking position. Put your weight firmly forward and hit the turn. As you finish the turn, edge firmly, bending your knees to absorb the force. Be careful that you are not edging unevenly. Often your outside leg will wander off, indicating that you are rather better at getting an edge on the outer ridge of your feet than the inner, arch, side (*see* canting, page 26). Try not to turn too much. End each turn pointing slightly down the slope rather than across it. On ice it is the complete edge that counts rather than just the heel. Unfortunately for beginners, the snowplough turn is useless on ice.

The good thing about ice is that there is usually a way round it. If you come to a field with lots of ice, pause before you go down. By looking around you may be able to see a way through. Quite often there is good snow left under the shadow of trees which frequently fringe the *piste*. Sometimes, in an icy mogul field, it is the sides of the moguls which are frozen solid, but the channels between them still contain reasonable and skiable conditions.

Other Problems

All this advice will not make you ski everything, but it will help. The main thing is to watch other skiers, particularly the experts. You might even manage to overcome those two terrors of the ski slopes, the gunbarrel and the rutted *schuss*.

The gunbarrel is a country trail probably used by horses in the summer. In winter, with a steady flow of skiers, it becomes a semicircular channel rather like a domestic rain gutter. The gunbarrel may run for a hundred yards or more, straight downhill, and is more than a little intimidating. If you are skiing it with snowploughs, do not go straight down the middle; it will be too icy and the arc will prevent your edges from connecting. Turn from side to side of the barrel, bouncing from one to the other. If you must do a straight plough, do so along the outer ridge of the barrel—the snow will be better there. Alternatively you can side-slip down the outer rim of the barrel, controlling your speed by edging, but this requires fairly good edge control. More advanced skiers will either short swing down or, if they are very confident, *wedeln*.

The rutted schuss is a fairly regular phenomena in resorts where there is a long straight final run to the base station. You will find it late in the afternoon as the soft snow freezes again. Make sure as you *schuss* that you have a measure of V-edging. A slight knock-kneed position in such conditions will produce the V and keep you steady. Avoid going into a snowplough.

Ski clinic

As soon as I get up any speed I just sit down in the snow. I simply cannot learn.

Lack of confidence in the early stages of skiing often results in the skier leaning further and further into the mountain until he falls backwards and simply sits down. Try building up your confidence by going to the baby lift, usually a simple rope just outside the village. There you will find slopes which will not be too steep or daunting for you. Do not try very much more than straight running; when you do this, experiment with relaxing. Flop your arms to your side, bend your knees up, and then down. Lean over first one way and then the other. Try a little hop now and then. Gradually you should find that your skis are not as dangerous as you subconsciously feel they are.

Try as I might, I cannot make a turn in the snowplough position.
Almost certainly you are giving up in the middle of the turn. This is where that basic rule of skiing—leaning out from the mountain—comes into play. Keep your weight on the outside ski, point your outer knee emphatically at the ski tip. Make sure that your inner leg is not straightened as you do this.

When I traverse my uphill ski starts to go higher than my lower. What am I doing wrong?
You are putting *all* your weight on the lower ski instead of most of your weight. So much emphasis is placed on weighting the lower ski that sometimes it is overdone. Ease a little more body back over that top ski—but don't overdo that, either!

Now that I am going faster and trying stem-turns I seem to have lost the ability to weight my skis properly.
Your eagerness to stay steady at speed means that you are bending forward from the waist, with your nose getting nearer and nearer your ski boots. Your bottom is sticking out behind. Raise yourself straight and bend your knees. Even try sticking your pelvis for-

ward. Then you will find your weight under control. You'll look smoother, too.

When I complete a turn I always swing into the mountain and find myself facing the wrong way.
You are not looking down the mountain when you finish your turn. As you come into the fall line fix your eyes on something down the mountain, perhaps another skier, a tree or a hut. Keep your eyes on that object until you are fully round the turn. Never look at your skis, and never look up the slope. Watch other skiers learning their first turns and you will see them suddenly twist their bodies into the mountain. That is what you are doing.

You tell me to unweight, but I can't really do it.
Every time you find yourself on a smooth straight run, try a little hop, lifting the tails of your skis off the ground. When you land, bend your knees. Gradually, as you get used to this, try hopping slightly to one side first, and then the other.

Well, I've tried that and I still can't unweight enough to bring my skis together in the stem christie.
Carry on with the hopping exercise and try and find a small mogul field. Do your stem christies over a gentle mogul, bringing your skis together as you come down the outer face of the hump. Are you sure your bottom isn't still sticking out?

I have tried very hard, but I cannot make the change from stem-turns to parallel skiing.
Get a good instructor. It is worth spending a little on private tuition at this stage, as it was in the very first few hours of lessons. If it is a long time since you learnt the stems, try a lesson on short skis; you will be surprised at the difference. Make good use of the moguls and try never, never, to relax back into old habits. Do not despise the gentler slopes—what you need is long, speedy, but not too steep, descents. This will build your confidence and allow you to think about what you are doing without worrying too much about whether or not you can handle that tricky stretch ahead.

My skis keep digging into deep snow.
It is possible that you have your weight too far forward, but more likely that your skis are unsuitable for these conditions. Skis, particularly some offered to recreational skiers in France and Switzerland, are too 'hard' for deep snow skiing. You really need some nice floppy equipment—Head GK 03, Kastle CPM 70, Rossignol Haute Route, Yamaha Floater or Millers will be fine unless you choose to go really fast on ice after your excursion into the deep snow.

I cannot hold my skis on ice.
Your skis are too soft, or tired, or the edges need sharpening. Have your equipment checked. If it is in good condition and you are determined to ski hard packed snow quickly, rent harder skis— Rossignol Stratos, Fischer Super GT, Kastle CPM TI 4000, or Head GK 05.

What if I want to ski both regularly?
Get combi skis. Popular ones are Rossignol Cobras, Head GK 02, Kneissl Magic 1000, Kastle CPM 50 (although the CPM 70 has now been modified to give it combi characteristics too) and the Atomic Rider.

Cross-country touring

When a downhill skier descends a mountain he may feel like a bird. Sometimes he realises that he is a caged bird, caged by the limitations of the ski runs, the lift systems and the fact that he is surrounded by other skiers. To discover ski touring is to escape this cage. It is to return to the original concept of skiing, the ability to make journeys of considerable distances with relatively little effort. It is a style of skiing which was out of fashion for half a century, regarded by some as a silly sporty remnant of the Victorian era. But gradually, as people have grown to look once more to the open

Each winter thousands of skiers take part in the annual Engadine ski marathon in Switzerland. For some, of course, it is a deadly serious competition. For most, however, it is a magnificent 35-mile romp, the object being to beat your friend—with a bottle of wine as a side bet.

spaces, to appreciate the calm of a snow-filled vista in the country-side, touring has come into its own again. It is one of the fastest growing leisure pastimes today, and is likely to remain popular for a very long time.

Touring and cross-country is known by its German title, *langlauf*, or as Nordic skiing. Normally the words 'cross-country' would imply a fairly active and fast style and 'touring' would mean the sort of perambulation which is the equivalent of country walks and which is what most recreational skiers do. I hope purists will forgive my blurring the definitions by using the term 'cross-country' for both.

The joy of cross-country is that the basics are so simple to learn. If you already have the elements of downhill skiing, that is the confidence on skis rather than the techniques, you will only need a morning of tuition before you are off on your first tour. It is not desperately exhausting provided you keep to your own pace. Cross-country skiing is very much like walking. If you break into a trot or even a sprint every now and then you will get tired a lot more quickly than if you merely walk along. Once you are used to it, you will be able to cover tens of miles in a day without very much fatigue.

The secret of cross-country skiing is that a ski naturally goes forward when it is pushed, but prefers to stick to the ground when it simply has weight on it. This movement can be encouraged by the right waxes on the soles of the skis in the same way as it can be dis-couraged for downhill. The skier uses this basic principal to make progress by a series of kick-off steps and glides—first one foot and then the other. The technique looks quite elegant and moves you along very rapidly indeed.

Equipment

There are four broad areas of equipment for cross-country skiing, three of them—mountain, general and light—in the touring class; the fourth is racing. Differences between the forms of skiing can be strong: in mountain touring you will need to carry a load on your back and speed is not the first requirement; racing, of course, is just the opposite.

Skis The first thing you will notice about touring skis is that they are narrower, side to side, than their downhill equivalents, and slightly thicker top to bottom in the vertical section. Cut in half they form more of a square than downhill skis. Normally they are made either entirely of one wood or of a complex lamination of spruce and other woods; there have been recent experiments with other materials but, as yet, none superior to wood has been found.

Most Nordic skis are very soft at the front end, to give you an easy ride through the snow, and very hard at the tail, to ensure precise direction control and aid the 'kick and glide' technique. As with downhill skis, the Nordic ski is arched so that if you were to place it on the floor you would see light under the middle section. This is to ensure that when weight is placed on the ski it flattens on to the snow and does not bend downwards to dig unevenly into the trail. Since your main objective is progress forward rather than a series of tight downhill turns, the skis for touring are usually a little longer than for on-*piste* skiing. Stood vertically, they should be above head height, and head plus three inches or so is normally recommended for people of average weight.

Although ski touring skis are very much cheaper than downhill equipment the beginner is advised not to rush out and buy them before he has tried touring. There are as many arguments over touring skis as there are over downhills. You should get to know a little about the sport before investing any money in what might be the wrong equipment. In the better known touring centres it is possible to rent skis.

Bindings Cross-country and touring ski bindings are completely different from those used on downhill skis, mainly because the heel must be kept free. As you walk, the rear half of your foot comes up from the ground as in normal walking, but the ski remains flat. The idea of cross-country ski bindings is that they should grip only the toe tip of the boot. Because of the flexibility of the boot there is often a rear binding on the lighter equipment which holds the boot straight when it is flat on the ski. Sometimes this device has an added attachment to make the hold permanent for a spell of downhill running. For general movement your binding will have

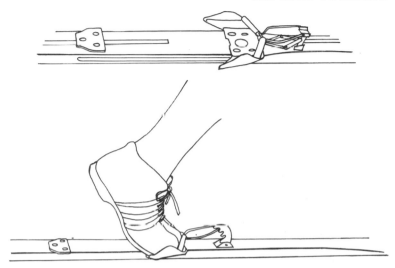

Cross-country bindings.

a light metal toe fitting, and a sprung cable which passes around the rear of the boot.

Boots Touring ski boots vary according to the type of work that is required of them. They are not the hard uncompromising type used on the *piste*. Cross-country boots look like hefty tennis shoes and are about as light. The light touring boot is more akin to a good strong walking shoe, and the normal touring footwear is about the same weight as the lightweight football boot.

Sticks Sticks are rather more important to Nordic skiing than they are to downhill. They must be light, since you are going to carry them over long distances, but they must have both the strength to push you along when necessary and enough 'whip' to give you a spring action. To give added drive, tips are normally set at a slight angle to the main stick. You will use fairly long sticks (armpit high) for the active cross-country, and a little shorter for normal touring.

Waxes Good waxing is crucial to good ski touring. Once you are initiated into the more closely kept secrets of the Nordic ski business, you will enjoy its intricacies. The ski soles are waxed to give them the right type of performance in the snow of the day. A simplified wax kit will give you three types of wax for three broad types of snow, and with these you should be able to ski without problems in most conditions. However, if you want the optimum performance from your skis, you will take a much closer interest in waxing; there is plenty of guidance available (*see* Bibliography).

Clothing Touring ski clothing must be warm, give the skier complete freedom and yet allow the skin to breath. Since falls are not a major feature of ski touring, there is less concern with waterproofing the upper body garments. Unless it is likely to snow, woollen and cotton knits will do. Heavy anoraks are usually far too sweaty for normal use, unless the weather is very cold indeed or you are going very high. A light anorak or thin single-layer parka will be enough. You may find that you prefer touring in a sweater; particularly if the weather is pleasant. You can always tie your outer anorak around your waist when you don't need it.

Usually touring skiers wear trousers that end just below the knee, with knee-length socks. Downhill stretch ski pants are not really suitable for touring because they offer too much resistance to the normal walking movement.

Other equipment The longer your tour, the more you will have to carry. This will include additional waxes, some food, a few tools for running repairs, and spare ski tips which clip onto a ski if it breaks. You might even be carrying camping equipment. Obviously you will need some form of baggage which will range from the simple 'bum bag' used by many downhill skiers to a small rucksack.

Nordic glide.

The Technique

The technique of touring skiing is natural and smooth. It will not be a strain if you are of average fitness and coordination. Because it is certainly much easier than downhill skiing, touring is a very popular family pastime.

Diagonal Stride The basic movement of ski touring is the diagonal stride, so called because of the exaggerated movement of the opposite arm to the leg which is being pushed forward—the power line is thus diagonally across the body. Start the movement from a. normal walking motion, in which your skis are gliding gently along the snow. Swing your right leg forward using a small, but quick, bending of the knees to give yourself added spring. Simultaneously swing your left arm a little above shoulder height in front of you. Your weight will be heavily on the left foot until the stride has been almost completed. With a slight final kick, enter the glide phase with all your weight transferred to the right ski. Do not extend this glide for too long or you will have to strain to bring up your speed again. As you move into the next stride, avoid jerkiness and try to maintain a steady progress. If you get into a brake-accelerate-brake motion you will waste a lot of energy. Try to relax completely in the glide position, and avoid weight transference until your rear foot has returned and overtaken the other foot.

Double poling This is a useful technique if you are going down a gentle slope or want to increase your speed. Bringing both skis together, throw both arms forward to shoulder height and place the stick points in the snow with the sticks vertical to the ground.

After a few simple lessons most people can acquire the basic techniques for ski touring. It's much easier to learn than downhill skiing, and much less damaging to the pocket. With a little practice and the right terrain tens of miles can be covered elegantly, and pleasurably.

Wait until you are nearing the sticks and then, bending your knees and hips, drive yourself forward. Do not apply weight too soon; pulling yourself forward with the stick is tiring. Simply push, glide, reach, glide, push . . . rhythm is the vital ingredient.

Double pole stride Combining the last two manoeuvres, the skier uses longer glides; he can only use this technique on a fairly smooth terrain. Instead of swinging one pole forward with each stride, you swing both. The longer glide is necessary to give you time to do this without unbalancing, but the double pole action should give you the extra speed necessary for this glide. Unless you are extremely fit, you will not be able to keep this motion up for very long.

Turns On flat terrain the touring skier will use 'skating' turns. Approach the turn with your skis together, transfer your weight to the outer ski and 'push' it away with a skater's motion, transferring your weight to the inner ski at the same time. As you come into your required direction, you bring your feet together again and centralise your weight.

Uphill you can incorporate step-turns into a normal diagonal glide technique, and downhill it is possible to use the stem-turns and stem christies. Nowadays you rarely see the original touring (and even on-*piste*) turn, the Telemark, in which the skier neatly curtsies into the snow.

Another useful touring technique is the 'herringbone' climb as described earlier for downhill skiing.

Racing

People who live in the lowland countries of the world rarely get the opportunity to see just how spectacular and exciting ski racing can be. The television stations in Britain, Belgium, the southern and eastern United States and Australia cannot spare the resources necessary for proper coverage of ski racing for what they consider to be a small audience. But watch ski racing either from the slopes or from your armchair in Austria, France, Germany or Switzerland and you will feel the excitement surging through you even faster than the schnapps.

There are three types of alpine ski racing, and different length races for Nordic cross-country. The three alpine categories are downhill, giant slalom, and slalom. In the downhill you come straight down the mountain, or at least straight down a prepared run. There are no 'gates' and you are fighting the clock. The speeds attained by downhill racers are remarkable. It is possible to reach well over 161km per hour and 113-plus is not unusual. To see a skier handling such speeds is both a thrilling and shuddering experience.

The giant slalom is half-way between downhill and slalom. There are gates, but the turns are not fiercely tight; the accent is once more on speed. This type of racing combines the need for a rapid movement with fine ski control and balance.

When the world's top skiers are competing in the downhill—in this picture on the slopes at St Moritz, Switzerland—speeds above 70mph are not unusual. But the skills of the racer are not totally removed from those of the beginner. Note how this competitor's knees are bent, not his body, how he is pushing forward down the fall-line, and how he is actually looking where he is going!

The slalom uses much tighter turns in which the skier is sent through gates, which are poles with flags on top. The skier must pass through these gates in the correct order. Coloured flags, normally red and blue, will tell the racer whether the gate is meant as a right or left turn. Skiers are allowed to hit the poles of the gates with their bodies, but their skis must pass between the markers. The art of the slalom and giant slalom is to take as direct a course as possible, shaving the gate poles and avoiding tight, slowing turns.

Main events of the ski year are the World Championships, the European Championships and the normal national races and Grand Prix. Famous race names in the calendar include the Arlberg Kandahar and the Kandahar-Martinin Citadin races, which are particularly close to the British heart. In the United States a very exciting professional ski circuit developed in the early 1970s. It has skiers competing directly with each other, skiing in pairs down

Racing turn.

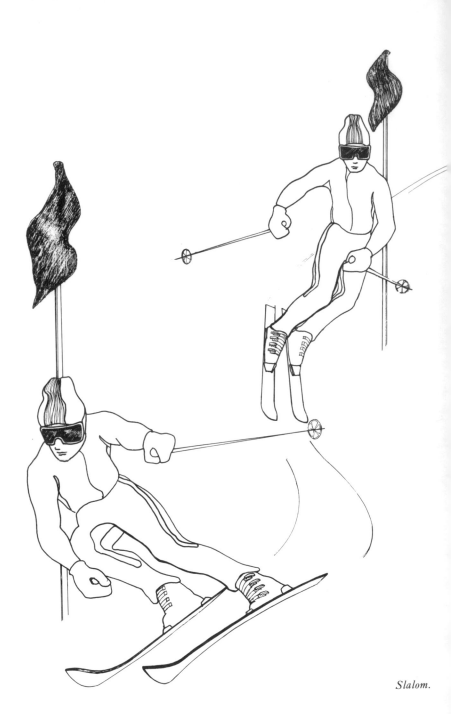

Slalom.

similar runs with fifty gates and three jumps in a quarter-mile course. This spectacular development involves sponsorship and large sums of money. Benson and Hedges and United Airlines have been major sponsors of U.S. ski racing.

Apart from skill, the vital extra component in ski racing is the wax that each team uses on the ski soles. Waxing racing skis, where every micro-second counts, is a highly specialised art. Competitors and team officials seen bawling and arm-waving at each other after races are most likely arguing over whether the correct wax was used. Waxing is usually left until the last minute, to get just the mix to make the skis pass as rapidly as possible over the snow. A wax that makes a ski move on ice will produce drag on soft snow, and vice-versa. But snow textures can change over the length of a race run, so what wax should be used? A good waxer is worth five to ten places in a fifty-competitor race of the top standard. No wonder tempers get short when the wrong wax is chosen.

In Europe, most villages have their own races and medals are normally awarded to holidaymakers who complete the set course in a specified time. In America, they use the NASTAR (National Standard Ski Race) system, which was introduced in 1968 by *Ski* magazine. NASTAR racing could possibly come to Europe. It would be very welcome, since it gives each skier a handicap similar to golf handicaps. Every skier's standard is compared with a national 'best' and, via a computer, he is given a rating and a pin indicating his standard. A gold pin means the male skier is within twenty per cent of the national standard time and the female within twenty-five per cent. You race against your own handicap to try and improve it. (My own NASTAR rating is embarrassing enough to be kept a secret.) The heart of ski testing for the U.K. is the Ski Club of Great Britain. Full details of the SCGB's tests can be found in Appendix 4.

CHOOSING A RESORT

Whatever your needs on a skiing holiday, the choice of a resort is a problem which can shuttle your thoughts between pleasure and despair. Trying to please everyone in a ski group is beyond the wit of most men. The swingers want discothèques, the relaxers want a peaceful village; the *piste*-bashers want miles of prepared runs, the deep snow addicts want freedom to roam; the gourmets want delicate flavours and soft lights, the gourmands prefer hearty meals and plenty of them. Just as skiing in each different country tends to have its own atmosphere, so resorts tend to vary enormously in mood. There is the jollity of Austria, the bustle of Italy, the modernity of France and the informal efficiency of America. The world of skiing is yours to choose from, but making that choice is by no means easy.

In narrowing it down, it is best to decide on a country first. Two main factors will come into this: the cost, and the general ambience of the ski resorts. If you have a low budget and are only interested in downhill skiing you will, for example, give Norway a miss. If packed beer cellars and rollicking *après-ski* are your idea of the good life, you would choose Austria instead of France or the United States. Seekers after the simple life might look to the lesser known resorts of Spain.

Having chosen a country, the selection of a resort is a question of poring through the brochures. In Britain, most of the major tour operators offer a wide selection of resorts which they hope will

Resorts differ considerably in style from country to country. Flaine (above) is a modern French development ; Söll (below) is a cosy old alpine village in Austria.

appeal to all tastes. If you read the resort descriptions carefully, you should get some idea of the mood of the village. The British Trades Descriptions Act forbids any false superlatives, so you are unlikely to be told lies, but make sure you realise what has been left out of the brochure copy. If it does not say there is a skating rink, it's no good complaining after you get there because you thought all resorts had them.

Make sure that you know, as accurately as possible, what the tour is going to cost. It is not the fault of tour operators that inflation throughout the world has sent ski prices rocketing; but the fact that this inflation continues to have an almost weekly impact means that nowadays the brochure prices of various operators are not necessarily directly comparable. With currency values changing constantly and oil prices fluctuating, current brochures tend to carry the date at which they went to press and thus the date on which their costings are based. The later this date the more accurate the price is likely to be.

When choosing your operator, consider the flight times. You may get an extra day's skiing (particularly if you have your own equipment) from an operator who flies out to a resort area in the morning and back in the late evening, as compared with one who flies out in the evening and back in the morning. And yet both are advertised as seven night tours! It also helps to get a map of the village to which you are thinking of going. Most national tourist offices can supply these. The map will tell you *before* you actually make your selection exactly where the hotel is in a resort—whether you have a long walk to the ski lifts, or the night clubs. Some tour operators supply hotel location details to travel agents so that you can check them there.

Your holiday will be that much better if some snow falls while you are there; it is a pity that snow conditions are very much in the lap of the gods. Generally speaking, any true resort should have snow in January and February (unless you happen to be in the

To ski in deep powder snow is to sample the ultimate in winter sport pleasure. This is the powder of the Rocky Mountains in Colorado, U.S.A. But even when the snow is good, other pleasures call . . . mountain top après-ski drinking in Switzerland.

southern hemisphere where the seasons are reversed). If you are skiing at Christmas or even earlier, you would be well advised to choose a resort which has a reputation for early snow, or is way up in the mountains, above 1,500 metres. The same arguments apply to skiing late, perhaps at Easter.

Some resorts, particularly in France, the United States and Japan, have snow-making equipment. Artificial snow is produced by pumping fine droplets of water into the air from a hose; the droplets freeze and fall to the ground as snow. This expensive machinery can usually provide a skiable run from November to April but it cannot, of course, cover a whole mountain.

Austria

There can surely be no doubt that Austria is the home of modern popular skiing. It was the delight of Tyrolean villages, combined with prices once the lowest in Europe, which brought visitors in their thousands to the ski runs and the *schuplatter* evenings. A great many lowland skiers in Europe today probably took their first faltering steps on skis in some Austrian ski school. Times have changed since those days of the 1950s and early 1960s. Austria's growing prosperity has strengthened its currency against those of its neighbours, making the cosy villages a little more expensive.

Austria is no longer cheap, but it is still very good value inasmuch as the visitor usually gets what he pays for. Its hotels and restaurants are surely unrivalled for their friendliness and waist-swelling food. The wine and beer flow, the songs resound through the villages, and the snow hangs charmingly from the eaves of the houses. Austria is probably nearer to the postcard ideal of what skiing is really all about than any other country. New hotels in the mountains are cunningly designed to look as if they were three hundred years old. They may have central heating and modern plumbing, but they often look from the outside as if they were fresh from the pages of some seventeenth-century story book.

For this reason Austria is still one of the best countries in the world in which to be initiated into the world of skiing. Against that sort of back-drop it is difficult not to enjoy your holiday, even if your boots do pinch a bit and the first snowplough turns are not coming as easily as you expected. After all, once your day on the slopes is over you can always retreat to the *konditorei* for a comforting slice of cream cake and a steaming cup of glühwein.

Austria boasts some of the finest skiing in the world; indeed the Austrians would claim that it is the best by far. Certainly there is a very wide range of ski areas and of resorts within those areas, from the elaborate ski circuses of the Arlberg and Kitzbühel to the as yet unspoiled villages of the East Tyrol. If there is a drawback, it is that the very popularity of some resorts and the enthusiasm for skiing of the Austrians themselves mean that the slopes can get very crowded at weekends and peak holiday seasons. Some may say, of course, that this only adds to the fun.

Austrian enthusiasm for skiing is legendary. Twice in the past twenty years, the nation has been chosen as host for the winter Olympics, with Innsbruck as the centre for the Championships. No visitor to the country can avoid noticing the passion the Austrians have for skiing, both as a sport and as a leisure pastime. Ski racing is followed on Austrian television as closely as soccer, cricket or baseball in other countries. For children in the mountain valleys, skiing is part of the school sports curriculum, and local junior champions are nursed along in the hope that they will emerge as triumphantly as such heroes as Karl Schranz, Toni Sailer and Anne-Marie Proëll.

The creation of such champions is of more than romantic interest. The village which produces a medal winner finds that much of the glitter rubs off on custom for local ski lifts, hotels and ski schools; the magic of champions is all pervasive. At a national level, the importance of Olympic and World Championship victories is obvious. If the Austrians are supreme, an image of good ski instruction is conveyed to the world's winter holiday-makers.

It was perhaps the very quality of instruction which set the seal on Austria's success in the winter sports business in the post-war period. During the 1950s and 1960s, the Austrians perfected their new teaching techniques and made skiing a much simpler and more enjoyable sport for the beginner. It is a pity therefore that they have been slow to capitalise on the more recent swing to short skis which has tended to give the less prominent ski countries an edge in their ski teaching image.

Personally, I would still choose Austria for the first-time skier. Given reasonable snow conditions and pleasant company there is surely no way in which someone going to villages like Alpbach, Serfaus or Ischgl can escape becoming totally addicted to winter sports. These are the Christmas-card resorts of Austria's western provinces, with a friendliness and intimacy which is rarely matched elsewhere.

At the time of writing, hotel rooms and meals cost much the same as they do in provincial Britain. To those accustomed to summer holidays in Spain, however, the price of drinking, particularly spirits, will seem high. A jug of glühwein will cost two or three times as much as the same quantity of sangria in the sunshine. Night clubs and discothèques tend not to charge for entrance but will load the drink prices instead—and Austrian taxation helps boost the cost even more. Of the main ski countries, however, Austria remains one of the least expensive for *après-ski*, dearer perhaps than Spain and the American west, but certainly cheaper than Switzerland, France and Norway. To make comparisons with Italy is impossible since there are as many changes in the value of lira in a year as there are twists in a bowl of spaghetti.

You must beware of extras in Austrian hotels. A room with bath usually means just that; it does not follow that there is a private lavatory as well. If your room does not have a bath or shower the hotel will charge for the use of the communal bathroom, and sometimes charge quite heavily. It is not unknown, but probably rare, for Austrian hotels to charge for water served with meals. Take your own soap—sometimes it's there, sometimes not.

Austrian hoteliers began to take tourists for granted a few years ago and won themselves a bad reputation. Two or three indifferent seasons (for the hoteliers) changed that and now the welcome tends to be more like it was in the good old days. To stay in a well-run Austrian hotel or pension, where the owners take a real interest in their clients, is to discover something you will find nowhere else in the ski world—the friendly conviviality of old-time skiing.

Most of Austria's ski villages are low lying, set among meadows that have been grazed for centuries.

There are literally hundreds of villages in Austria from which it is possible to ski, probably a hundred or so which would lay claim to being ski resorts, and perhaps fifty to sixty worth the effort of booking into for a week's skiing. As far as the foreign tourist is concerned they are concentrated in mountains which overflow from Switzerland and start petering out beyond Salzburg. From Brand in the west, to Filzmoos in the east they offer a fascinating range of skiing. The fact that these resorts are based on living communities, and have not been carved out of the mountains for the benefit of the ski community alone, means that Austrian skiing has the edge on some of its rivals in terms of beauty. The hills are dotted with little farmhouses and you will often ski past sheds and hear the tinkle of cowbells, telling of occupants patiently awaiting the spring. Much of your skiing will be down trails cleared through the trees. The lift systems in Austria are rarely adequate for really busy seasons; if you are a dedicated *après-skier* or sunbather by all means book a holiday for Easter, but if you want to ski choose a time when the queues and the car parks are a little less packed. It is surely time that ski resorts were licensed to sell only a limited number of valid lift tickets per day. It borders on fraud to sell a skier a ticket which costs upwards of eight pounds for a week and then tell him he has to queue for fifteen minutes every time he wants to take a chairlift.

Austria's best known international resorts are Kitzbühel and those in the Arlberg region, centred on St Anton. Both offer some of the finest skiing in the world, together with extremely sophisticated night life. 'Kitz' is without doubt the most glamorous of the Austrian resorts and a place to spot the stars. The fact that it offers so much—and is priced accordingly—makes it a resort that should be avoided by first-time skiers, although dedicated non-skiers will find lots to occupy their minds.

But in some ways it is a pity that Kitzbühel has so strong an image for its *après-ski*, because the skiing itself is amazingly varied. The skiing is in two areas, the Horn and the Hahnenkamm. Both are served by cable cars which can get a little crowded in peak season. Once at the top it is the Hahnenkamm which offers the most varied skiing, with a baffling array of runs which should keep any skier busy for a few weeks without becoming bored. This is very good territory for the third or fourth year holiday skier who is beginning to want something to test his skills. If you feel really confident the Hahnenkamm offers some splendidly steep runs. The nicest way down to the bottom at the end of the day is via the 'Fleck', but that means getting a taxi back to Kitzbühel. The 'Standard' is a pleasant enough alternative, and takes you through woodland to the cable car station.

Less experienced skiers might prefer the Horn, which boasts a complex of simpler runs, and helps to separate skiers who would otherwise simply get in each other's way. There are some excellent nursery slopes at the Trattalm. It is on these slopes that the visitor is first likely to meet the famous Red Devils of Kitzbühel—the ski instructors. There are more than two hundred, all of whom seem to speak passable English. The Kitzbühel school is very good indeed; nevertheless I would not recommend Kitz to the beginner, simply because a resort of this kind can be a little overpowering. It's like getting your first introduction to alcohol from Napoleon brandy—splendid, no doubt, but hardly worth the expense.

There are some pleasant enough resorts within striking distance of Kitzbühel which will cost a great deal less and give the skier a chance to dip his toes into the waters of Kitz for the price of a rented car or bus ticket. Westendorf is the nicest of the satellite resorts, but it is also the furthest away from Kitz itself. This village is an excellent choice for the beginner, with its pretty houses, gentle nursery slopes and active night life. Nearer to Kitzbühel are Kirchberg and St Johann, and both Söll and Fieberbrunn are within striking distance. In this area I would choose Kitzbühel for the ski enthusiast, and Westendorf for the mixed group or beginner. The one great advantage of Söll is that it is nearer to Munich airport than any of its rivals, an important point if you don't like spending too much time in buses.

Kitzbühel's jet-set rival, St Anton, is the crowded, active, happy, irritating, unchallenged heart of Austrian skiing. The village is one in which the local authorities fight a vain and unending battle against the motor car. Much of the centre has now become a pedestrian-only area, which is pleasant once you are a resident but awkward when you are arriving or departing. The ski school is reckoned by many to have no rival, but has the ego-crushing technique of relegating any visiting skier a couple of classes below his professed standard—and then proving that the ski school knows best. Ski the easy runs at St Anton and you will be happy on the trickier *pistes* of lesser resorts. The beginner will receive the very best of instruction, but will find that the nursery slopes are not easily accessible.

St Anton's major drawback is that the lift system, complex as it is, cannot cope with the crowds. Efforts are being made to overcome this by opening up new facilities for the Gampen runs and a completely new area to the south of the resort, the Gamberg. I skied there at Easter 1975, getting some good skiing and a sunburnt nose for my trouble. The Gamberg gives St Anton much of what it needs—good intermediate ski terrain. The runs of the Valluga tend to be on the challenging side, but once you have skied the Valluga and the Galzig you can really claim to have skied the best.

St Anton's other ski area, the Gampen, has a reputation for being a little easier, but the first-timer might be forgiven for failing to notice the difference in standard.

At night St Anton really comes to life with an incredibly wide range of evening entertainment which starts off with tea dancing. The shops offer a dazzling array of goods, but the prices are high. Remember before you go that St Anton is one of the world's top ski resorts and you have to pay for the privilege of being there.

St Christoph is the twin resort of St Anton. It is just as pricey as its big brother but in some eyes has one or two advantages. Since it is smaller it has an intimacy which St Anton lacks. You not only have access to the St Anton ski areas but can also rest happy in the knowledge that St Christoph's snow tends to be a bit more reliable and, perhaps most important of all for the beginner in a group which is otherwise expert, it has easily accessible nursery slopes.

A little further away from St Anton are two villages which would come high in any list of Europe's best in their own right—Lech and Zürs. Lech is a near-perfect resort for the first-time skier, with plenty of room to practise and an excellent ski school. Somehow it has managed to keep its village atmosphere in spite of considerable recent growth and offers not only the basic ski runs, but also more testing slopes. Zürs is a ski paradise with some really superb terrain. The two villages also provide one of the longest and most fascinating runs likely to be possible for a first-time skier after a week or two in ski school: Lech-Zürs on the Rufikopf side of the valley. From there the beginner would have to take a bus back, for the Zürs-Lech run via the Madloch is slightly trickier.

Other resorts in the area include Ischgl and Galtür. Ischgl is much the most interesting, since it provides much of the sort of skiing which is perfect for the two-weeks-a-year leisure skier.

Independent travellers who have difficulty finding rooms anywhere in the Arlberg (St Anton, Lech, Zürs), or the Paznauntal (Ischgl, Galtür) might consider staying in Landeck, which has some skiing of its own when the snow is right, but is also within half an hour's drive of the major resorts of the area. Determined *piste*-bashers can even drive to St Moritz. Landeck is a largish country town which can offer any non-ski members of a group rather more than most ski resorts in the way of bigger shops, restaurants and non-skiing activity.

The disadvantage of skiing by car in Austria is that parking facilities range from dreadful to non-existent and the search for a parking space can often consume hours which would otherwise be spent on the slopes.

Resorts you might also find mentioned in the brochures include Alpbach, Bad Gastein, Brand, Gargellen, Gaschurn, Hinterglemm, Hintertux, Igls, Ischgl, Kaprun, Lermoos, Mayrhofen, Nauders, Niederau, Oberau, Obergurgl, Saalbach, Seefeld, Serfaus, Sölden, Söll and Zell-am-See. Ski resort judgments are inevitably subjective. My favourites among this list are Alpbach and Serfaus, although neither of them would suit the really demon skier who wants challenging black runs from breakfast till tea-dance. Both are cosy little compact villages, although their differences serve to illustrate the problems in choosing a resort. In Alpbach the better skiing is a long way from the village—much further than a healthy walk—so you have to rely on a shuttle bus service which can be inconvenient if you decide to start skiing late or finish early in the afternoon. The Serfaus lifts are much closer to the village centre, but the village is sadly lacking in night life and a very long way from Munich airport. Alpbach is definitely the choice for singles who have no intention of staying that way for the whole holiday, and Serfaus for loving couples or family groups.

If you are of an age where everyone in the discothèque these days looks as if he or she should be in school then Seefeld is a good choice. Always popular with the British, Seefeld is a solid, almost self-satisfied resort with some excellent restaurants, and night clubs which tend to attract a more mature clientele. The ski runs provide agreeable but unchallenging intermediate sport: Seefeld is also a centre for cross-country skiing; if you have never been on cross-country skis this resort offers an ideal baptism.

Mayrhofen is an extraordinary spot. Ernst and Erika Spiess have made the ski school one of the best in Austria, and it has a particularly good reputation for teaching children. For some Mayrhofen is too crowded; for others it would not be the place it is without the crowds. There are few places I would sooner be on an alpine evening than Mayrhofen, but there are simply too many hotels for the lift system. The skiing is good, particularly for beginners, on the Ahorn and Penken mountains, but although I have been to the village half a dozen times there has never been enough snow in either area to ski from the top right down to the village. More challenging skiing can be found at nearby Hintertux—and you don't try skiing down from the top of that complex unless you really know what you are doing. It is all steeps, gullies and tracks cut through the trees. The leisure skier is better advised to take the gondola back.

You can get much more detail about the villages from the Austrian State Tourist Office (*see* Appendix 2). The *Avis Guide to Skiing in Europe* has comprehensive descriptions of most of the better-known Austrian resorts and is very helpful. A much broader spread is contained in Mark Heller's *Ski Guide to Austria* which is useful if your choice lies between several of the smaller villages. The trouble with books is that they are heavily salted with personal opinion, no matter how hard the authors struggle against this, and most of the writers are keen skiers. Use books to get an idea of what you want, but the best way of finding the resort that suits you is to seek out personal opinion. Generally speaking, however, places are as nice as the people you meet, and the skiing is as good as the snow you find.

France

Until fairly recently the French kept their skiing very much to themselves. One or two of the alpine resorts were known to the outside world but foreign traffic into France was very limited, and even today very few non-French skiers penetrate the ski areas of the Pyrénées or the Massif Central. Although France has one or two 'first generation' resorts, such as Chamonix, which have grown up from existing villages, much of the development has been more recent. First came the great post-war developments of Courchevel and Val d'Isère, and then the explosion of new projects with their ultra-modern architecture and runs designed to give the holidaymaker the maximum amount of skiing with the least effort —resorts like Flaine, Les Arcs and Isola 2000.

French skiing has a very distinctive flavour, and anyone who is expecting Paris on ice is in for something of a disappointment. As you travel from resort to resort in France, you will discover probably the most consistently high standard of ski terrain in the world. There is excellent ski instruction, particularly in those resorts which teach *ski évolutif*, the system which employs a gradually increasing length of ski while the skier is gaining confidence and ability. You will also find acres of high ski runs, often way above the tree line, where the snow is dependable and the lift systems supremely efficient. The French have organised their skiing very well indeed; often they provide parking facilities which can cope with all but the most hectic of weekends and ski lifts which can usually handle peak season crowds. The hotels tend to offer good value, particularly if you take full pension, and the food in the ski villages is good. I am not sure that the French have yet come to grips with the problem of mountain-top catering in the sense of offering a quick, inexpensive, lunch-time snack, but for evening dining they are unrivalled.

The major complaint heard about French skiing concerns the French themselves. As a nation they do not mix particularly well with foreigners. Salt a room full of people with French and they will soon sift themselves into a little group apart. And they do tend to scramble a little in the lift queues. The lone English, German or American visitor who does not speak the language will stay lonelier in France much longer than in Austria or Norway.

Above all the French resorts are ideal for easily accessible, varied intermediate skiing, a facility rivalled only by the Rocky Mountain resorts of the United States. But the American resorts are tailored more for the occasional intermediate skier than those of France. For someone who wishes to get full value from a weekly lift pass, France must be the natural destination.

French skiing really came into the headlines in the 'sixties, with new fashions in turns which temporarily outshone the Austrians and their ever popular *wedeln*. Today the rivalry between France and Austria in the field of competitive skiing is as strong as ever, but the differences in teaching techniques are gradually disappearing. In a French ski school nowadays you will be taught either by the *ski évolutif* method or by a shortish ski traditional technique which may be slightly more aggressive than that taught in Austria but is otherwise the same. A disadvantage is that you may have difficulty finding instructors who speak any language other than French.

One of the reasons for the British lack of knowledge about French skiing in recent years has been the high cost of holidaying in France. But as British inflation has roared ahead so France has come to seem a little less pricy than it used to, and today offers, if not bargain basement holidays, reasonable value.

Most skiers want to go to the Alps, and I will concentrate on that area; you would need more reasons than skiing to wish to visit ski resorts elsewhere in France which do not have the facilities, the ease of access and the snow reliability of those in the alpine region. Most package tour companies will deliver you to Geneva for your entry airport, although if you are going to Isola

2000 then the airport will be Nice. From Geneva you face a drive of between thirty minutes and three hours to reach your resort. The early part of the road is very good indeed, but the deeper you get into the mountains the less reliable your timetable will become. The valleys of the French Alps are highly susceptible to winter fog, although the ski stations themselves are usually far too high to be bothered by such conditions.

The independent skier has very good access to French skiing via a variety of routes. Although I have done it a few times, I would not recommend trying to drive to the main resort areas from Britain in one day. There is an hour's time difference during the winter months which sets you back from the start, and you reach the mountains just as you are tired and the conditions are at their worst—narrow mountain roads and, hopefully, snow. Digging a car out of a snowdrift in the early hours of the morning after an all day drive from London can put a strain on any beautiful friendship. Much simpler, but more expensive, is to fly to Geneva and rent a car at the airport. (Avis and Hertz both provide skiers' cars there, with snow tyres, chains and ski racks.) There is a good train service from Paris to several of the alpine towns and an Air Alpes scheduled air service will take you to Courchevel, although the flights are often fully booked, particularly at weekends.

If you do choose to drive in your own car remember that you will need snow tyres and probably chains. If you fit snow tyres in the U.K. it means observing the low speed limits for such equipment for hundreds of miles. It may be cheaper and less frustrating to drive your own car to Lyons and then rent a ski car locally—or better still, buy a package in the first place.

France's best known resorts are Chamonix, Courchevel, Megève and Tignes/Val d'Isère—all of them totally different. Chamonix is probably the most complete 'town' of them all, with a well-established atmosphere. Its grand buildings, which date back to an age when Chamonix first became a fashionable mountain resort and a centre for climbers (which it still is), give it an air of comfort and stability. The town itself sits at the foot of Mont Blanc and is perhaps a little short of sunshine until the sun gets a bit higher towards the end of February. In the grey days of January Chamonix does not appear the most attractive of resorts, but the skiing is absolutely superb and up in the ski areas above the town itself there is usually sunshine in abundance.

Chamonix is certainly not a resort for the beginner, and you should go there for your first winter sports holiday only if you are forced to do so by more determined members of a holiday party. The ski areas are scattered about a long valley and there are limited facilities for the novice.

One of the most spectacular cable car trips in the world starts from the centre of Chamonix. You can travel up from the town in two stages to the Aiguille de Midi where the views of the Mont Blanc community of mountains are memorable. There are few places where you will feel more on top of the world, with snowy ridge after snowy ridge disappearing into the distance against a backdrop of deep blue mountain sky. From the Aiguille du Midi you can go on further by gondola to the Gare Helbronner and the Italian frontier. The run from there to the valley has a fairly comfortable middle section, but both the first and final stretches can be a bit intimidating.

There are several other ski areas close to the town: the easiest to reach is La Flégère, which has the added attraction to lazy-bones like myself of being sunny, south-facing, and relatively easy going. La Flégère skiing is so pleasant that it is easy to forget how tired you are, a fact of which you will be sharply reminded if you try the tricky run back to the valley. But skiers who prefer the sterner stuff will turn to Les Grands Montets, the ski area reached from Argentière. The snow tends to be better on these runs and the skiing itself much more testing.

Les Trois Vallées, with its three resorts Courchevel, Méribel and Les Menuires, is a complete contrast to Chamonix. One of the oldest of the 'new' resort areas, it sprang up in the years after the Second World War. There are nearly two hundred miles of marked runs, enough to keep the most enthusiastic skier content for many a ski holiday. Although a little on the expensive side, the resorts of Les Trois Vallées provide a lot of well-planned skiing for the money. Perhaps because it is purpose-built, a large proportion of the runs are designed to meet the greatest demand—medium standard *pistes* for the holiday skier who wants to enjoy his winter sports and not spend his time fighting the elements and the slope.

Courchevel 1850 (there are a series of satellite resorts with other numbers which indicate the height above sea level in metres) is very much a jet-set resort. Here you will find the best of everything in skiing, from snow to fashion, but you will pay a price for it. Many British visitors seem to prefer Méribel, whose skiing is linked with both Courchevel and Les Menuires (you can buy a lift pass covering all three areas), and which has been built in an attempt to recapture some of that old world atmosphere. As one tour operator's recent brochure put it, 'the slightly conservative skier can enjoy Courchevel skiing without having to brave the Gallic hordes'. The ban on high rise buildings helps to give the place its intimate atmosphere, but the same ban also accounts for the fact that you will find it easier to get chalet accommodation than hotel beds in Méribel.

Les Menuires sees a return to the concrete block style of development so popular in latter-day France. It is easy to condemn this type of resort, but the layout is very convenient for both skiing and *après-ski*. There is little of that tiresome marching about the village carrying skis, and plenty of covered and heated shopping and restaurant arcades for after-ski loitering. It is much more pleasant to seek out company for the evening ahead in the warmth of these arcades than in the chill of a ski lift line.

Another resort which is excellent for the once-a-year skier is Megève, with its well-protected traditional buildings and a ban on motor traffic after lunch-time. Megève, for all her age, is still something of a deb in her attitude to winter sports. Her eyes are turned to the fashion pages as often as to the ski slopes and the watching crowds are likely to be as interested in the cut of your salopettes as in the grace of your *avalement*. There are few better places in the world to enjoy some graceful, or even frenetic, *après-ski*, and if your wallet is of the right thickness you will do it in some pretty trendy company—or maybe trendy, pretty company.

To get the full use of the wide range of skiing in and around Megève will cost you well over twenty pounds a week (1975 prices). You ski not only from Megève itself, with its four ski areas linked by bus, but also in resorts such as Chamonix which is not far away. In the morning it is very pleasant indeed to ski Le Jaillet which gets lots of early sunshine and where the snow lasts well, although that description does not apply to the lower slopes of the area. If conditions are right you can take the very rewarding 12km run down from Le Jaillet to the nearby village of Sallanches. The Mont D'Arbois area on the other side of the village is much more extensive; it provides good skiing for intermediates and experts on the upper slopes and, lower down, some of the best nursery slopes in France. The Rochebrune runs also offer a good mixture, and are served by a particularly fast cable car which delivers you to a nest of drag lifts. If you feel really daring you can take the Emile Allais black run back down again—but there are simpler routes.

If Megève has a lighter side in its attitude to skiing this is less obvious at Val d'Isère and its sister up in the mountains, Tignes. These resorts are almost totally dedicated to skiing and the *après-ski* is something of an afterthought. Reaching Val d'Isère is not the easiest of tasks since it involves a somewhat tedious drive up into the mountains from Albertville via Bourg St Maurice. If the weather is bad the journey can be miserable, and it is not helped by roads which are often pitted after a hard winter's wear. But, for the keen skier, the journey is well worth the effort. There are miles and miles of simply superb skiing from the Glacier de Pissaillas at one end to La Grande Motte at the other. The village itself is not pretty—I prefer to stay in Tignes or Val Claret which for all their modernity have more warmth—but the mountains are unbeatable. The skiing is in two broad sections, the Bellevarde and Tommeuse, both of which give access to huge interlocking networks of runs, and offer a mixed bag of standards. The snow is reliable at the top for a very long season; indeed, you can enjoy summer skiing in July and August. The *après-ski* is better in Val d'Isère itself than in the other resorts, which suffer from the usual problem of centres which are dominated by apartment accommodation—the flat-dwellers tend to stay at home in the evenings rather than go out on the town.

Not far from Val d'Isère is Les Arcs, one of the dozen or so new resorts which opened in France in the late 'sixties and early 'seventies. Les Arcs, a village of novel wooden architecture clustered above Bourg St Maurice, has become the European centre of short ski tuition under the direction of Robert Blanc. It is one of the best places in Europe for those who are absolutely determined to ski in a relatively short period of time and should be especially recommended to those who feel that they will 'never ski' because they are not particularly athletic or feel themselves too old to start. I have met many a skier who has learnt the sport after retirement, and recently attended a race prize-giving where one of the winners was eighty-four.

Which of the newer French resorts you choose, including Les Arcs, is very much a personal selection. Resorts like Isola 2000 are nearest the sun, while those like Flaine are very convenient for the airport. Flaine is a classic of the modern genre, with its giant concrete buildings and brilliantly designed lift system. Once you have skied in one of these new resorts you begin to yearn for the *après-ski* of Austria or Switzerland, but you also become adjusted to a standard of lift systems which makes those long-established ski regions seem very old-fashioned indeed. The new resorts are ideal for groups of skiers who are going to make their own fun back in the apartment or their hotel rooms in the evening. They are not particularly pleasurable for individuals or for non-skiers.

The French Government Tourist Office (*see* Appendix 2) in London is one of the most helpful, although it can be extremely difficult to reach by telephone. A letter or a personal call will prove less frustrating.

Switzerland

To many a British mind the very word Switzerland means winter sports. The ski resorts of St Moritz, Davos and Grindelwald were as much part of the fashionable scene in the 'twenties and 'thirties as the Astor and the Ritz. Well, those days have long since gone and Switzerland has to fight for its ski custom with more practical weapons than the simple call of fashion. But it has these weapons in some abundance, for Switzerland arguably has more household name resorts per Alp than any other nation in the world, and their familiarity is justified. They do have one major drawback, however, and it would be foolish not to mention it—expense. Skiing in Switzerland is not cheap even for the Swiss, which is why so many of them head for France. For visitors from the U.K. and the U.S.A. who have seen the value of their pounds and dollars fall disastrously in recent years the price tag can seem very high indeed.

There are ways of cutting costs in Switzerland, and the ever helpful Swiss National Tourist Office is eager to tell people about them, but any comparison of like with like in terms of accommodation is likely to come out unfavourably for the Swiss.

However, a great many people think that the quality of the skiing is such as to justify the expense, and that quality is very high indeed. The Swiss ski villages are usually year-round resorts set in very active local communities. They therefore have a completeness which other areas lack. They feel as if they have been there a long time, unlike the ski transit camps which have sprouted in some parts of the world, bustling from Christmas to Easter but like ghost towns in May and June. This feeling of permanence is present even in the newer stations like Verbier.

One of the great advantages of the Swiss resorts is that most of them are very easily accessible. There are year-round international airports at Geneva and Zürich, a very good train system which serves many of the resorts, and roads which are kept clear of snow in the worst of weather conditions.

For the independent traveller who wishes to see a number of resorts by far the best way to tour is by train. The Swiss rail system is efficient and will take you where you want, when you want. If you are travelling around by train you will save a considerable amount of money by buying a Swiss Holiday Pass for eight or fifteen days. This gives you the freedom of the tracks and takes away much of the worry of moving around; you can buy either a first or second class pass. If you are doing a lot of travelling, be prepared to change trains several times on some of the more complex journeys from resort to resort.

Perhaps the problem with Switzerland's image is that people

immediately assume that Swiss skiing is St Moritz and Zermatt repeated dozens of times throughout the mountains. The glossy resorts of Switzerland still lure the fashionable and the rich—the two are not necessarily the same—and there are times when you will have to fight your way to your hotel through Lamborghinis and Porsches. But there *is* another Switzerland, a world of friendly little villages with cows in the main street, where the not-so-rich Swiss (and there are a few) themselves ski; and even in the glamour resorts the growth of a fifth column of younger skiers has produced a different style of entertainment and accommodation.

Above all, in Switzerland you will find comfort and quality. That cream cake may cost you a little more in Gstaad than it does in other resorts, but it is likely to be superb. And what is true of the cream cakes applies to the skiing. The resorts tend to offer excellent ski facilities, though some doubts have been expressed about the overall standards of Swiss ski instruction these days (with notable exceptions like Davos, which emphasises *ski évolutif*). One of the particular attractions of Swiss skiing stems from the fact that Swiss skiers seem to be very much creatures of habit. The slopes appear to empty magically for a few hours after midday as the locals make off to do justice to all that Swiss cuisine and alpine sun. The skier who forgoes this pleasure will find much shorter lift queues and more *piste* to play with—and I still think you get a better tan skiing than sitting in a deck-chair.

St Moritz and Zermatt probably share the honours as the world's best-known ski resorts. But, as with Switzerland as a whole, we have now probably reached the stage where this reputation is counter-productive; as many people are deterred by the very idea conjured up by the names as are attracted by them. The two resorts are completely different.

It is terribly easy to forget that St Moritz won and retains its reputation simply because it offers absolutely magnificent skiing. The rich and beautiful may seem to be rather free with their cash, but in fact they generally want to see a touch of quality in their purchases. There may be times when St Moritz looks like the Boulevard St Germain with icing sugar, but towering above it all are mountains with an impressive variety of runs. It is this skiing which attracts the crowds, whether rich and beautiful or down-at-heel and a little care-worn. And it is probably the best ski resort in the world for offering a combination of ski and non-ski attractions. If you have the money to do it in style, St Moritz is the near-perfect destination for a family group which has one or two members who have no intention of ever getting on skis. St Moritz can let its hair down, but the higher you climb in the cost bracket the more formal life becomes. Generally that formality will express itself in its stylishness rather than an adherence to convention, but you will still find restaurants and hotels where you will be quietly ushered away if you are not wearing a tie. Lower down the social scale you will find life more relaxed and as ear-splittingly lively as anywhere in the Alps. St Moritz's twin resort of Pontresina is perhaps a little less overwhelming than St Moritz itself but getting the most out of the skiing is difficult unless you have a car.

One of the great attractions of St Moritz is its good sunshine record. If you really want to get a deep tan to impress your friends on return, spend a few days in March skiing the south-facing Corviglia runs. The skiing here is generally fun, open *piste* stuff, but there are more testing opportunities. If you prefer relaxed skiing beware of the fact that the runs tend to interweave with each other and, although there are signposts, you have to take care not to wander off on to something which is a bit more difficult than you thought.

Sometimes the Chantarella-Corviglia funicular can get a bit crowded, and you will save time by reaching the slopes from Celerina, a route which does not have the same attraction as the funicular for non-skiers.

If skiing is taking priority over a quick tan you will probably prefer the Corvatch slopes, which provide some fantastic skiing on north-facing runs and have a reputation for powder snow. True powder is outside the experience of many European skiers, particularly those who have learned in low-lying Austrian resorts during the recent mild winters. It takes some getting used to, but once you have mastered the art it will be difficult to drag yourself away from the Corvatch runs if the weather is right.

Quite apart from any other attraction, if you want your holiday pictures to be instantly recognisable by skiers and non-skiers alike there are only two resorts in the world where this is nearly guaranteed—Zermatt and Cervinia. Both share the Matterhorn as a backdrop, Zermatt on the Swiss side, and Cervinia in Italy to the south.

Although as well-known as St Moritz, Zermatt is really only a skiers' resort. You cannot take your car into the town, but instead must make your way there by train from Tsach, a few miles down the mountain, where all motor transport has to be left. The absence of cars—horse-drawn cabs are offered as an alternative—lends Zermatt an away-from-it-all atmosphere which is unique but which can be trying for someone who is not going to ski. This is particularly so since a non-skier is not going to find much company. Zermatt boasts little in the way of beginner or even lower intermediate skiing and those of that standard will probably face the chore of coming back down the mountain by funicular because the runs back are too difficult. This is a frustrating and expensive hobby.

Zermatt really comes into its own as a place for the young dedicated skier, preferably with a fairly deep pocket. Just about everything in Zermatt is of the best—the skiing, the hotels, the restaurants, the night life, the shops. Little is cheap, but you are unlikely to come away feeling cheated—unless you expected a budget holiday with easy skiing.

For nearly twenty years people have been expressing concern that Zermatt, which first sprang to fame as a summer mountaineering centre (which it still is), would outgrow its village atmosphere 'soon'. Perhaps that day has already arrived, but visitors now will find a mixture of old and new which is not unpleasant and which can probably grow a little more before the magic is finally destroyed.

The skiing is in three areas—Gornergrat-Stockhorn, Blauherd, and the Schwarzsee with its access to the Matterhorn itself. Each of the areas has its attractions. The Gornergrat provides the best beginner slopes that Zermatt has to offer, and also affords a pretty good chance of sunshine. Better skiers can take some of the very long runs down to Zermatt, but there are some fairly testing sections en route. The Gornergrat area connects with the Blauherd, which has a wide selection of runs of various standards. Unfortunately the base stations of all three areas are widely separated and you will need the horse-drawn taxis to ferry you about.

During your stay you will almost certainly want to ski across to Cervinia in Italy, which you can do by taking the lifts up to the Theodulpass on the Schwarzsee side of the village. But set aside a whole day for the visit, and don't forget your passport!

Zermatt is one of the points on the famous *haute route* transmountain ski journey from Saas Fee to Chamonix and Verbier and you can join it here for a part-section trip. You will need a little experience of ski touring before trying this one, but Zermatt itself offers considerable opportunities for gaining the necessary skills. It might be best to practise touring on one visit, and join the *haute route* trek on the next.

At the risk of upsetting those who have a soft spot for Gstaad, I think that the resort which bites closest at the heels of St Moritz and Zermatt in the reputation stakes is Davos, a large town which would never win any prizes for beauty but which has the Parsenn as the most glittering jewel in its five-pointed ski crown. Davos arguably has the best skiing and the best ski school in Switzerland —but such is the subjective nature of both debates that I would prefer not to argue on either point. In Davos—or rather near Davos, since nothing could actually be 'in' such a sprawling conglomeration of hotels and apartment blocks—are the areas of the Rinerhorn, the Pischa, the Brämabüel/Jakobshorn, Schatzalp . . . and the Parsenn.

A full description of these areas would take up a book in its own right. Briefly there is no way in which a skier of any standard is going to exhaust the opportunities of Davos within the normal two-week holiday period. To twist a well-known quotation—when a skier is tired of the slopes of Davos, he is tired of life. As for the town itself, perhaps I have been too damning. It certainly offers every facility you could want, but it is not the sort of place you are going to fall for the moment you arrive. Instead Davos is really a place to meet people. And if you meet nice people you will have a great time there because there are very few hours in any day when the town does not offer something for everyone. Every time I have met people who say they enjoyed Davos, apart from the skiing, I have found that they had a great social life. When people say they hate it the root cause is usually that Davos was the scene of the end of some beautiful friendship.

If you are tempted by the ski attractions of Davos and want to stay somewhere with a little more charm, then less than ten miles down the road is Klosters, a fashionable little charmer with extensive skiing of its own and within striking distance of its big neighbour. Your holiday will not cost less in Klosters, but you might find it has more eye appeal than Davos.

Two other resorts with considerable charm are Mürren and Saas Fee. Mürren is as typical an alpine village as you will find in Switzerland and has long been a favourite with the British. Because it is a family-oriented resort it is a bit short of *après-ski* facilities but is lively enough to have been used as the setting for much of the James Bond film *On Her Majesty's Secret Service*. Saas Fee is set high in the Valais and has delights which are best sampled in the early spring when the sun has had a chance to take away some of the chill and chase out the shadows which hang about this pretty little resort in December and January. It is totally relaxed and unsophisticated and one of the best bets in Europe for late season skiing.

Elsewhere in Switzerland I would choose Adelboden, Champéry, Lenzerheide, Leysin, and Villars for beginners and intermediates who want something of the mountain atmosphere for their holidays; Andermatt, Arosa, Engelberg, Grindelwald, Gstaad, Verbier, and Wengen for those who are looking for a little more challenge from their trips. Of the latter, and Andermatt and Engelberg would make good choices for the enthusiastic skier who also has to take his or her family along. Crans-Montana, a two-in-one resort which overlooks the Rhône valley, claims to be one of the sunniest ski resorts in Europe. You'll probably get a tan there; you'll certainly find good skiing; but it's all a bit soulless.

Italy

Analysing the mood of Italian skiing is as difficult as defining the nature of the Italians themselves. There is probably a greater variety of resorts in Italy than in any other ski nation—the big and the small; the pretty and the downright ugly; the sophisticated and the simple; the organised and the anarchic. Perhaps it has been this difficulty in attributing a character to Italian skiing that has helped to keep out foreigners over the years, for it is only in the relatively recent past that the Italian slopes have seen much of a foreign invasion. There are hundreds of Italian villages which boast some form of uphill transportation, but the average non-Italian's knowledge of the country has extended only as far as having heard of Cortina, Courmayeur and Sestriere—and that's about all. It has been the efforts of foreign tour operators, and not the Italians, which have brought such villages as Sauze d'Oulx, Macugnaga, Ortisei and Madonna di Campiglio to the attention of the ski world.

If there is any continuing theme to be found in Italian skiing it must be zest. The sheer determination of the Italians to make the most of both their skiing and their *après-ski* shines through almost every aspect of an Italian ski holiday. Mostly this simply adds to the fun, but it can all be a bit tiresome on a sunny weekend in an overcrowded resort which is too close to Milan or Turin. Italians can lose their cool when the lift lines are over-long or they can't find a place to park their cars.

There is a tendency for the Italians to ski the way they drive, with a certain amount of bravado. On the whole, the *pistes* are designed for this. They are usually extremely well maintained, but favour the more competent intermediate skier. An added disadvantage for the beginner is that ski instruction in Italy is erratic. You'll come back either loving your instructor or in total despair; and English is not as widely spoken as it is in Austria or Switzerland. Italy is a great place to ski once you have discovered the basic rules of the game—on and off the slopes.

Italian resorts are the same as the Swiss—but for different

reasons—in that they are very much quieter over the lunch period. The Italians are tremendous weekend skiers and love to pack into their resorts from Friday afternoon onwards, taking long, leisurely and alcoholic lunch breaks. The foreigner spending two weeks in the more popular resorts at peak season would be advised to concentrate his skiing on weekdays and weekend mealtimes.

The airports which you will normally use to reach Italian ski centres are those of Turin and Milan, although Venice is sometimes used for the far eastern resorts, Munich for those closest to the Austrian border, and Geneva for those near to Mont Blanc.

The best-known of the extreme westerly resorts is Sestriere, a village built for skiing and conceived in the 'thirties as another brainchild of the Fiat Agnelli family. Today Sestriere's buildings have a style which clearly reveals their age. The town may not have instant eye appeal, but it does offer a considerable range of amenities and a wide choice of superb skiing served by an excellent lift system. Sestriere is extremely popular with the better-off Italian skier and is not the cheapest of places for a winter sports holiday, but you get what you pay for and you will have to travel a long way to find superior ski facilities. The skiing is in three main areas, the Sises, which offers some fairly steep but open skiing, the Banchetta, where the visitor will find the greatest range of runs including some longish, 7–8 km *pistes* down to the village, and the Fraiteve, which in itself is limited but provides access to both Sauze d'Oulx and the steep Rio Nero, one of the best-known runs in Italy. Any visitor worth his salt ought to ski the Rio Nero before he leaves; there is a drop of more than 1,500 metres in the 8km journey.

Apart from Sauze d'Oulx, whose good intermediate slopes and compact village make it probably the best resort in Italy for the novice with two weeks' holiday and no car, the other resorts of this area include Pragelato, Chiomonte and Bardonecchia. All are fairly simple villages which principally cater for the local trade. A better bet for the foreign visitor is the twin resort of Claviere (Italy) and Montgenèvre (France), which straddles the border. It has an excellent snow record, but to get the full advantage of the amenities you will need your passport.

Further north on the Franco-Italian border is Courmayeur, an absolutely delightful little town with charming houses and cobbled streets. Courmayeur, which sits at the southern base of Mont Blanc and atop the Aosta valley, has been the centre of mountain life in the area for centuries, and any visitor immediately feels this sense of tradition. The mood is Italian with a strong French accent, a mix which has been cemented in recent years with the building of both cable car and road tunnel connections with the French resort of Chamonix. In the spring it is possible to ski over into France via the Gare Helbronner.

The fact that Courmayeur does not offer a wide range of skiing to the *piste*-basher has probably helped it to retain much of its charm. It is an extremely attractive resort for the intermediate and has a long ski season, at least at the top (the village itself is fairly low and so can lose its snow in a mild spring).

Further down the Aosta valley, which now runs alongside the Swiss border, is Breuil-Cervinia, and the mountain shared in this case is the Matterhorn. To enjoy Cervinia to the full you ought to be well beyond the snowplough stage, although there are some nursery facilities. Most of the skiing is either on broad, open runs which give you a nice flattering feeling when you are trying to perfect your parallels, or on short, sharp, but fascinating drops which will really test your style. There is, of course, access to the runs of Zermatt (passport needed) and you can buy Zermatt lift tickets in Cervinia. The night life is active, but the shopping facilities are somewhat limited. Cervinia is an ideal resort for the second- or third-year skier, and there are few more spectacular places to obtain a suntan.

Not far away as the mountain eagle flies, but a very long distance if you use the roads, is Macugnaga, a resort much used by British package tour companies and one which leapt into the headlines a couple of years ago when it was cut off by snow for more than a week. There are two villages to the resort, Staffa and Pecetto, a short bus ride or a fifteen-minute walk apart. Perhaps better known as a delightful summer walking retreat and mountain climbing base, it is only in the past four or five years that Macugnaga has become well established as a ski resort. It has changed a little in these years, but not enough to spoil it; you can still have a pleasant and relatively inexpensive holiday there. But it is not really ideal for a first-timer or for someone who wants to ski every daylight hour. What Macugnaga does offer is a nice relaxed retreat for someone who has skied before and wants some enjoyable, not too testing, sport in charming surroundings.

Another resort heavily used by tour operators is Madesimo, popular partly because of its proximity to Milan. The Milanese pour into the village at weekends and disappear late Sunday afternoon. It is a very attractive resort and, although quite large it is compact enough to be enjoyed without too much walking. The skiing is all on the north-facing slopes of the valley and is better for skiers with at least a little experience.

Livigno is a duty-free zone tucked away in a corner of Italy that pushes like a jigsaw piece into Switzerland. When you arrive you will have some difficulty in deciding where the village starts and where it ends, because it wanders seemingly for miles along the road. At one time the village was a strange no-man's land which could be reached only by a hair-raising drive up from Bormio, a drive which could take hours despite the fact that less than thirty miles separate the two places. Now there is a tunnel to Switzerland and the impact of this new access to civilisation is beginning to show already. Like the village, the skiing is spread along the road and a car is a very useful asset. Livigno is an attractive resort, and its attributes are best enjoyed by the beginner or second-year skier.

The old Roman spa town of Bormio is much bigger and provides rather more in the way of skiing. Late in the season the village itself sometimes loses its snow, but on the upper slopes of Bormio 2000 and Cima Blanca (Bormio 3000) the conditions are generally reliable until late in the season. The village has a quaintly traditional character which has so far survived the modernisation which is in progress, and it boasts an *après-ski* atmosphere which is almost worth the journey in its own right. In this area, however, I prefer Madonna di Campiglio, which has a wide range of skiing accessible by good uphill transportation from close to the resort centre.

Further east still we come to the resorts clustered around

Bolzano, most of them with names which are as yet unknown outside Italy—Campitello, San Martino di Castrozza, and Colfosco among them. Better-known are Canazei, Ortisei and, of course, Cortina d'Ampezzo. Cortina is Italy's 'great' resort by all the normal definitions of that word. The skiing is good, if scattered, the town is large and, in the height of the season, fashionable. The après-ski is hectic and can be expensive. And the scenery is spectacular. Cortina received international attention when it became the setting for the 1956 Winter Olympics, and since then it has grown considerably. There are four main ski areas: the Faloria-Tondi; which is reached by cable car and has some attractive intermediate runs; the Cristallo, a section which involves a long bus ride to the base station and is best suited for more experienced skiers; the Tofana, which has an impressive variety of lifts and runs of varying standards; and the Pocol, with direct access from the town and very good relaxing runs. I admit to a personal antagonism towards Cortina, for on the various times that I have been there the weather has always been bad. I have seen pictures of it in the sunshine, and actually met people there with deep tans, but my last afternoon in the resort was spent sitting in a café getting increasingly drunk on local wine while watching a steady fall of sleet tumble from an utterly grey sky. This was all the more irritating since the day before I had been thoroughly sun-scorched on the slopes of St Jakob, only a few miles away in the East Tyrol of Austria.

North America

The first place I skied in North America was in the Rockies of Colorado. We were a small group of enthusiasts setting off from London like an expedition to some extremely foreign shore. Somehow America and skiing did not fit our chauvinistic image of the sport. One of our party was . . . well, one of the most charmingly splendid bastions of the ski world. On our way out she confessed she was apprehensive. After all, how could the nation which had given the world Coca-Cola possibly compete with the

Parsenn or Les Trois Vallées? It was two weeks and many mountains later that we sat on the aircraft taking us back across the Atlantic. 'You know,' she eventually admitted, 'I don't think skiing in Europe will ever be the same again.'

Skiing in the United States and Canada, or at least in the western areas of both those countries, is certainly different from normal European skiing. The fact that so many Americans come to Europe, in spite of the expense of such a trip, is an indication that it is not necessarily better. But it is definitely different.

Defining this difference is extremely difficult. The area is so huge and the resorts so numerous that it is dangerous to speak in generalities but, risking that danger, there are a few points that can be made. From Canada's Jasper in the north to Taos, New Mexico, in the south, the North American resorts offer a much wider range of well-maintained beginner and intermediate resorts than Europe.

The snow, in the Rockies at least, is much drier than in Europe and the conditions are more consistent. In resort after resort you will find ego-snow—a perfectly manicured *piste* with a covering of fine powder which encourages you to travel fast and feel good. For the dedicated skier, however, all this can, after a while, become a little monotonous. The resorts have been tailored to meet the demands of the once-a-year skiers, and are sometimes short of the varied runs found all over Europe. But an even greater drawback is that many North American resorts are incredibly dull once the ski day ends. It is hardly surprising that Americans and Canadians are amazed by European *après-ski*. The basic reason for this lack of night life is two-fold: the abundance of apartments, and the frequent sprawling nature of the developments. Life can be quite pleasant if you have taken your own party, but difficult if you arrive alone.

The skiing of the east, particularly New England, is in many ways similar to that of Europe. Indeed, the (*Sound of Music*) von Trapp family settled in Vermont because it was so similar to their native Austria. Vermont's ski areas can be reached within a couple of hours' driving from Boston, and this accessibility encourages the crowds and can make weekends a time of long lift queues. In the depths of winter the area can also be bitterly cold, probably one of the most unpleasant differences that a European finds when he skis America.

Your first visit is likely to be to one of the better-known areas within striking distance of a major city. Mt Snow, in southern Vermont, would confirm many of your preconceptions about skiing in the country as a whole. Mt Snow has around sixty-five miles of ski runs and even with that amount of space still becomes somewhat overcrowded in peak season. The runs themselves are American classics. Throughout the U.S.A. and Canada you will more often than not find yourself skiing through the trees. The carving of broad ski runs through the mountainside forests gives these resorts their distinctive appearance. An American ski mountain looks as if it were erupting snow and pouring it down in rivulets through the pines.

But at least at Mt Snow you can rest your head within strolling distance of the ski lifts; often in the United States you need a car to get the most out of the ski facilities. Another popular eastern ski area is Lake Placid, New York, where the 1980 Winter Olympics are to be held. It is a large but scattered community which would be very depressing indeed unless you had your own transport— but with a car and good company, it provides more than enough skiing to keep the most enthusiastic occupied for a two-week holiday.

Frankly I see little point in a European making the trip to the American east simply for downhill skiing; he can get more and better on his home continent. The same is not true of the west, nor, probably, of the touring facilities of New England. Ski touring is a very fast growing sport in North America, and in New England there is a highly-developed network of marked trails linking lodges and farms which offer meals and accommodation. While the downhill resorts are frequently packed with New Yorkers *en masse*, the trails are a skiers' delight, solid with nothing but snowy silence. For someone who wants to try ski touring at its best the choice can only be between Scandinavia and New England.

For a European the main attraction must surely be the west, the incredible resorts of Colorado, New Mexico, Utah, Nevada,

California, Idaho, Oregon and Washington in the United States, and Alberta and British Columbia in Canada. Although there are hundreds of villages in these areas with ski-lifts of some sort, there are around seventy resorts in the west where the average European recreational skier would in no way be disappointed. I am amazed by the number of skiing businessmen who go all the way to San Francisco in the wintertime and do not seize the opportunity to ski the resorts of Lake Tahoe, which provide a complex of villages and slopes rivalled only by parts of the Tyrol.

The main gateways to skiing in the American west are Denver, Salt Lake City, Reno and Seattle, all of them served by America's main ski airline, United. There are packages available to some American resorts, but it is often cheaper in the winter months to take an Advance Booking Charter from Europe and book an on-going United package out of New York. If you are particularly well-heeled there are direct scheduled flights into Denver from London. As far as Canada is concerned (and my apologies to Ontario and Quebec, which hold romantic memories for me but must again be overlooked in deference to the Rockies), Calgary is the gateway. Air Canada operates packages out of New York and Toronto and, at the time of writing, is busily setting up deals direct from the U.K.

I must admit that I have not skied all the resorts of the Rockies, and will concentrate my attention on those that I have actually visited. The furthest south of these is Taos in New Mexico, and oddly enough this is the one with the village which comes closest to a European flavour. From the map Taos seems a most unlikely place to ski. It is on the same latitude as Rhodes and has an image of semi-desert Indian country. First impressions, as you drive in from Albuquerque, confirm this view, but gradually you climb away from the plain (where, incidentally, you see a crushingly poor standard of living) and into the snow.

The resort was created by Ernie Blake (a native of Frankfurt) and is a complex of ski lodges, set in craggy tree-lined scenery. Unlike many U.S. resorts this one has grown gradually instead of springing up overnight, and has an atmosphere to match. The skiing is at an impressive height, above 2,700 metres, and is mainly on the sort of powder snow which is rarely seen elsewhere in the world. Taos is not a big resort, and probably not the best choice for a two-week vacation for someone who has never been to the United States before, but if you get the chance it is well worth a visit. At least it is an introduction to the sort of names which are given to runs throughout the North American continent—Inferno, Bonanza, Pigsticker and High Noon among them.

More typical, and more accessible, are the resorts within driving distance of Denver, centres like Steamboat Springs, Breckenridge, Loveland Basin, Keystone, and those giants of the Rockies, Vail and Aspen. My first introduction to these areas was Steamboat, where the broad open runs—more than fifty of them—are served by a lift system which rarely sees a queue. Steamboat's *piste* maintainance is a revelation; its main drawback is the fact that the village seems to have been picked up by some giant hand and scattered around the valley.

But in Steamboat, as elsewhere in the Rockies, you will find that magical powder snow. Because the runs are so high, and the winds so dry, the snow tends to have a talcum powder nature which is extraordinary to ski. Once you have your powder legs you should really try the back bowls at Vail, the resort which houses the American famous, including President Ford, in the winter months. Vail is probably my favourite American resort, although Aspen comes a close second. The powder snow in the Sun-Up and Sun-Down bowls is quite remarkable and Vail village itself has a much friendlier atmosphere than many American resorts.

Aspen is a collection of several ski villages, all of them of a very high standard in their own right. Aspen Mountain, Buttermilk and Snowmass are all close to each other, and the advertised shuttle bus service actually works (and is free). Aspen Highlands, again served by the same bus service, is a bit further away and should be allocated a separate day trip. The Aspen complex will give you more intermediate skiing per week than any other ski resort in the world.

Further north are the resorts around Salt Lake City, home of the Mormons and some extraordinary drinking laws (which may or may not affect you, as they vary from resort to resort). Salt Lake claims to be the ski capital of America (a claim which mile-high Denver would dispute vigorously), and it does have a large number of excellent resorts within a very short driving distance of the city itself. Salt Lake's Mormons have never quite adapted themselves to the loose-living ways of the ski world but gradually the two are beginning to live with each other. The prime resorts of the area are Alta, Snowbird and Park City, of which I have skied only Park City. This is an old mining town which is high on atmosphere but low on night life in the European sense of the word. The skiing, once more, is open and powdery, with a commendable lift system and *pistes* which run through aspen trees down to a base station surrounded by a massive car park. Park City is typical of many American resorts in that it boasts 'well-groomed' runs which are equally allocated—one-third easy, one-third difficult, and one-third most difficult!

The foreign visitor to resorts such as this is baffled by both the lack of lift queues and the friendliness of the locals. After a couple of days of people approaching you and asking, 'Are you single?' you realise that it is not your marital status that is being questioned, but simply whether or not you are prepared to ride the ski lift with the enquirer. People are so delightfully approachable that it becomes almost an embarrassment.

Even further north there are some superb resorts, notably Jackson Hole in Wyoming, but by this time you are getting a bit too far from the gateway cities and the problem of travel for the European becomes a major one. But if you have a car, and the time and resources, you might investigate the resorts of Washington and Oregon—Leavenworth, Crystal Mountain and Timberline Lodge.

The British skier is likely to look at the Canadian Rockies which, like ski areas the world over, have advantages and disadvantages. The advantages are that you can often have the best of American skiing, with good lift facilities, superb snow and staggering scenery, combined with a more cosmopolitan approach to life than may be found in the western U.S. The main disadvantage is that it can be very cold.

Probably the ski experience of a lifetime is to ski the Bugaboos,

Cariboos or Monashees by helicopter. This is not cheap (at the time of writing about twenty-five to thirty pounds a day, including accommodation and helicopter) but it is unforgettable. It can all be a bit hectic; some tourists think the object of the exercise is not to enjoy themselves but to chalk up as many vertical feet skied as possible. Others are there simply for the pleasure of skiing virgin snow at impressive heights and amid breath-taking scenery. More down-to-earth are resorts like Marmot Basin (Jasper), Garibaldi and Banff. Marmot Basin seems to appeal most to European hearts as far as the skiing is concerned, although Banff probably has more to offer in the way of a complete resort. Banff's great advantage is that it is within easy motoring distance of Calgary. If you get the times right you can even go by train. Banff itself is a pleasant town and has the splendid old Banff Springs Hotel, a grand old lady who has yet to show her age.

Banff's skiing is at Mount Norquay, where there are good nursery slopes for the beginner and, for the more experienced skier, the very intimidating North American run from the top; Sunshine Village, a resort area approached by a fascinating shuttle bus ride and graced with probably the cosiest atmosphere in North America (possible exception, Taos); and Lake Louise, the most extensive of the three areas and one with a very strong English accent. Anyone who has travelled all the way from Europe would probably be best advised to stay in Banff and make day trips. If you must rest your head at a base station, choose Lake Louise.

For anyone with a taste for the outrageous in skiing, North America does offer a little more. There is skiing in Alaska, naturally enough, but also—surprisingly, perhaps—in Hawaii. In fact the mountains of Hawaii are very high, and the islands are a lot further north than many people realise. You can ski on the extinct volcano of Mount Kea at 3,900 metres, although you are requested to allay local nervousness by having a heart test first!

Europe

Skiing in Europe means a great deal more than the Alps; it extends from the slopes of eastern Europe to the highlands of Scotland, from the snowy lands of Scandinavia north of the arctic circle to the Sierra Nevada in southern Spain, only a few short miles from the sunshine beaches of the Mediterranean. The variety is, of course, enormous.

Scotland
Scottish skiing has really only come to the attention of the ski world during the past decade. There are three main areas: Cairngorm, in Strathspey, Inverness-shire; the Cairnwell above Glenshee in Perthshire; and Meall at Bhuiridh, Glencoe. Obviously in a country the size of Scotland there are dozens of places where it is possible to ski, and the gradual acceptance of ski touring is slowly opening up more of these regions, but for the downhill skier it is these three areas which offer the most.

Cairngorm is probably the best known of the areas, served as it is by the towns and villages of Strathspey and Badenoch and with its good access road from Aviemore. There are six ski lifts and the snow conditions are fairly reliable until quite late in the season. But Cairngorm suffers from the problem that besets much of Scottish skiing—the weather. There are times when the winds are high and the cold is bitter and the skier has to be thankful that Scotland is as famous for its whisky as it is for its snow.

Glenshee has five T-bars to the Cairnwell Mountain and two more to the slopes at the other side of the valley. Glencoe is probably the most popular of the Scottish areas; it attracts advanced skiers and is a major gathering point for Glaswegians at weekends. At the time of writing, however, parts of the lift system are only in use at weekends, so access to many of the runs is restricted.

Spain

Spain has only recently been discovered by the outside world as far as skiing is concerned. It boasts a surprising number of resorts and a surprising number of skiers who, like their resorts, were largely overlooked until they started winning Olympic medals. At the moment the foreign skier has probably heard of the resorts of the Pyrénées and of the Sierra Nevada. Not far north of Madrid, however, is the Guadarrama range which offers at least three resorts well worth a visit; and in the far northwest there are the villages of the Cantabrian mountains. Spanish skiing is still in its very early stages. The resorts tend to be simple when contrasted with those of the Alps, and lack the sophisticated infrastructure that surrounds rival ski areas. The fact is that many of the Swiss and Austrian resorts are based on fat little mountain villages which have long been prosperous from farming or trading. That is not the case in Spain. The mountain villages are basically poor and gradually being stripped of their populations. Skiing can sometimes be their salvation.

The focal point for many package tour visitors is Formigal, a new resort complex built above the old mountain town of Sallent. Formigal was built specifically for skiers and makes its own pleasures. The skiing is on broad open runs served by a really well-designed lift system. Late February and early March are probably the best times of the year to visit the area, although the snow can sometimes remain long into the spring. The weather in the Pyrénées is very changeable. You would be unlucky not to have a few days of really strong Spanish sunshine, but you might also have a period of dull, windy weather which can make Formigal a very chilly place indeed.

Not far from Formigal is the less well-known Panticosa, a tiny village with a couple of small hotels and one or two new apartment blocks. Panticosa is much more sheltered than its new big brother and can often provide pleasant skiing while Formigal is shivering in its winds.

There are several other resorts in the Pyrénées where the regular skiers would be amazed to hear any language other than Spanish or French, centres like Candanchu, Cerler, Masella and Nuria.

The foreign visitor is much more likely to find his way to Andorra, not Spain politically but very much part of the Spanish mood. This independent principality has some modest skiing at Soldeu, about twelve miles from the capital town of Andorra la Vella. When you are booking your accommodation be careful to choose the right place to stay. Soldeu is a pretty little place and pleasantly peaceful once the day trippers have departed at the end of the ski day. But it does not have the facilities, particularly the shopping facilities, of Andorra la Vella. So you either stay with the shops and travel daily to the ski runs, or do it the other way round.

At the other end of the Iberian peninsula is the Sierra Nevada, an area providing the sort of skiing that dreams are made of. You ski within a short driving distance of the Mediterranean, and frequently ski in simply scorching sunshine. During the drive up from Granada, you begin to wonder whether there will ever be any snow. But snow there is, and usually in great abundance until very late in the spring. It is not unusual in April to see people skiing in bikinis on broad treeless runs that start at around 2,400 metres. The building of facilities at the Sierra Nevada is proceeding apace; at the time of writing they are luxurious but limited. There is very little in the way of night life, so this is another of those resorts where it is best to take your own company.

Germany

You will find skiing in various parts of Germany, along its borders with Switzerland and Austria, but little has been heard about German skiing for the past few years—thanks to a series of particularly mild winters. Without a doubt, the most famous resort is Garmisch-Partenkirchen, a superbly maintained old town on Germany's southern border which lies at the foot of the huge Zugspitze mountain. One of the pleasures about planning a trip to Garmisch is that if there is no snow you can just carry on driving and be into the mountains of Austria in a matter of minutes. But if there is snow then Garmisch is a very enjoyable, if expensive, place to stay. The ski areas are fairly scattered so transport is useful, though there is a very good linking transportation service. The skiing on the Hausberg-Osterfelderkopf can be excellent for second-year skiers upwards. By all means go to the top of the Zugspitze to get a spectacular sight of the Alps. The view up there is fantastic. The skiing is not.

Norway
Norwegians tend to get very cross with the preconceptions other nations have about their skiing. We all seem to believe that there is no downhill skiing in Norway, that everyone in the country is ski-touring mad, that the days are short, and that it is very cold. The problem with refuting any of these ideas is that there is an element of truth in all of them. Norway is predominantly a ski touring country, but it does have some very good downhill resorts—Voss must surely rate among the better European alpine-style villages. The days can be short and cold if you choose to go in the very depths of the winter, but the Norwegian snow season stretches long into the spring, when conditions can be unbeatable.

The joy of ski touring is, of course, the fact that you can go anywhere there happens to be snow. If you are the escapist type you can head to the far north, into Lappland (but leave that trip until well into the spring); but for most visitors the villages of the south provide pleasures enough. All Norwegian ski resorts boast miles and miles of marked trails and it is relatively easy to rent ski touring equipment. The best-known resort is probably Lillehammer, a delightful town with superb facilities for touring and a modest amount of downhill.

The main downhill resort is Voss, which is best reached by train from Bergen. Voss played host to the World Alpine Championships in 1970, which should be proof enough of its downhill capabilities. The slopes are reached from the cable car up to Hangur. There you'll find the ski school and a restaurant where you can fortify yourself for the downhill runs. The skiing is not desperately challenging, but it will keep the average holiday skier occupied for the period of his stay. But if you visit Norway for skiing and do not try ski touring you will miss a great deal.

Not far from Voss is another downhill resort, Geilo, which is also on the Bergen-Oslo railway. This particular town has long held a special place in British hearts and you will find Anglo-

Norwegian kinship, which flourishes throughout Norway, at its strongest here. Geilo also has a reputation for its *après-ski*, considered to be among the liveliest in the country. There are seven ski lifts, and an amazing lack of queues. The only other downhill resorts which might tempt the foreigner are Hemsedahl and Norefjell, but there is a string of worthwhile downhill/touring centres like Fefor, Gausdal, Skeikampen, Wadahl, Dalseter and Spatind.

Other European countries
Scandinavia is a ski touring paradise and there are extensive facilities in Sweden and Finland. Ski touring is a major sport in the Soviet Union, too, including the woodlands around Moscow. However, for the moment at least, the Russians do not seem particularly keen to encourage outsiders to taste either their ski touring or their downhill facilities—at least, Intourist gives you a very blank look if you try to buy a ticket to a Russian ski resort.

The same is not true of other eastern European countries. In Poland you can ski the High Tatras, a spectacular area where the main resort is Zakopane. There is plenty of hearty night life and a cable car takes you to the top of the mountain which offers a lot of varied skiing.

Hearty night life can also be found in Romania, where the main resort is Poiana Brasov in the Carpathian mountains. But most western Europeans seem to prefer the jollity of Bulgaria or Czechoslovakia. The Czechs have several resorts in two mountain areas, the Giants and the Tatras. Špindleruv Mlýn is within easy motoring distance of Prague, but Starý Smokovec is probably more worth the trip. First-timers might try Strbské Pleso, where the runs are a little less testing.

The Bulgarian resorts tend to be very simple indeed. Vitosha is a gentle sleepy place with modest skiing and gypsy music to lull you in the evenings. Borovets, which is in the Rila mountains, is a little larger. It plays host to various competitive events and offers some longish runs. In this respect Pamporovo, well down towards the Greek border, is even better.

Yugoslavia will one day, I am constantly assured, overtake

Austria in the number of ski resorts it offers. There is certainly a considerable area of mountains on which to draw, but for the moment the Tyrol can rest in peace. Most foreigners seem to find themselves either in Bled or Kranjska Gora. Bled is not a ski resort in itself, but a very beautiful lakeside town. The skiing is in the mountain villages around, the best of which is probably Zaternick. Kranjska Gora is much more of a ski resort in the normally accepted international sense, with its night clubs, swimming pool and extensive lift system.

For those who are looking for something different in their skiing, in the sense of getting back to simplicity, eastern Europe offers a great deal. However, you should decide before you make your booking that it is really what you want. You can also find simplicity in Switzerland and Austria, but with it you will get fibre-glass skis, step-in bindings, telephones that work and superb ski instruction—just a few of the items not always instantly available in the east.

The World

The world of skiing does not end with the Rockies and the Alps. There are skiers in dozens of unlikely countries and far more ski valleys to be explored than ever have ski lifts today.

But outside Europe and North America the main concentration of ski madness is Japan. The Japanese take their skiing extremely seriously and each weekend from December to March can be found packing the roads and ski trains in a frenetic scramble to get to the snow. For much of the time there are lift queues which simply would not be tolerated in the western hemisphere, although that particular problem is not so severe in the Hokkaido resorts like Sapporo. Many of the resorts now offer western style accommodation, although a western skier is likely to find the whole scene a little bewildering.

The nearest resorts to Tokyo are places like Naeba and Shiga. Naeba has more than twenty lifts and a 4,000 metre downhill course which has a world reputation. Avoid it at weekends and in early season when the snow is unreliable, but otherwise a visit can be very rewarding. Shiga is even bigger, with a vast array of runs of varying standards and more than fifty ski lifts. There are dozens of other resorts scattered evenly throughout Honshu and Hokkaido. Most of them are of a very high standard, although there are rather a lot of single chairlifts around. If you intend travelling to one of the further resorts in order to avoid the crowds, my advice is not to drive. Japanese trains are excellent and comfortable, whereas driving long distances on Japanese roads can involve anything but comfort.

But if you fancy a taste of Pacific skiing and it happens to be July, you can always turn your eyes towards Australia.

Australian skiing began to come to life when the Austrians moved into the country in the late 'fifties. Suddenly there was a rash of ski schools and resorts. Australian skiing can be very good, and has the attraction for Austrian ski instructors that winter in Australia is summer in the Tyrol. The ski season normally starts around June, with the best conditions found in July and August. In September you can expect the sort of snow you get in Europe in late March and early April. Perhaps 'expect' is too strong a word. Australian weather conditions are notoriously variable and in some areas it pays to check first on the snow situation before you make the trip.

Probably the best skiing in the country is in New South Wales, at Thredbo, which provides the steepest skiing in Australia (but the runs are not particularly long by European standards). Also about three hundred miles from Sydney is Perisher Valley, a resort much more suited to beginner and intermediate skiing and where the snow conditions are considerably more reliable than the Australian norm. There is more beginner skiing close to Perisher at Smiggins Hole. There was an attempt once to link Perisher and Thredbo by chairlift, an attempt which was thwarted by foul weather conditions at such heights.

The resorts of Victoria may not boast such good snows, but they do have slopes a little closer to the main urban centre of Melbourne. Mt Butler is a big resort by any standard but still manages to get extremely crowded in peak season. A bit further away is Mt Hotham and Falls Creek, and there is some modest skiing at both Mt Buffalo and Mt Baw Baw. A major disadvantage to Australian skiing, apart from the uncertain snow, is the popularity of the sport. The slopes can be extremely crowded, and much of the accommodation is in the form of club lodges.

You'll find a little less crush and some excellent skiing at Mt Cook in New Zealand, and given the opportunity of taking some southern hemisphere ski time this would probably be the best choice. New Zealand also offers glacier skiing.

No investigation of the southern hemisphere should miss Chile. Portillo is the retreat of the American ski jet-set in the summer months. The resort is about two hours by car from Santiago and has a good cover of powder snow which is usually reliable from mid-July to mid-September. High in the Andes, most of the runs it offers are suitable for second or third year skiers, but there are a few real testers. On one of them an American skier exceeded 100 m.p.h. a few years ago.

Slightly lower speeds are normal many thousands of miles away in the Himalayas. There are one or two small ski resorts in India, and several places where you can ski virgin snow with the aid of a Land Rover and a driver willing to keep shuttling you up and down your chosen mountain. At Gulmarg, however, they actually provide lifts, and the skiing in this simple but adequate resort can make a pleasant break from the heat of the main Indian towns.

There are dozens of areas like this, in countries which most of us would consider hot, where there is good skiing. In Iran the sport has been catching on very quickly in recent years and this process is likely to accelerate. There is a considerable concentration of ski lifts between Ab-Ali and Polur on the peaks road to the Caspian Sea. These are small resorts, and somewhat better facilities can be found to the north of Tehran at Shemshak and Shahrestanak. To people who question whether the new resort being built in the Karaj valley will really prove to be something 'capable of competing with the most famous alpine resorts' the Iranians will simply reply: 'One should remember that Their Imperial Majesties are expert skiers.'

In many sunshine countries the skiers have to be not only expert, but also pretty quick off the mark. It snows most years, for example, at the 1,650 metre peak of Troodos in Cyprus, but the snow can be a bit variable and you must be ready to leap into your car and drive fast to the top in order to make the best of it. The same is not true of the resorts of the Lebanon, where there are one or two villages in which the conditions are really quite good.

APPENDIX 1
A Skiing Gazetteer

It would be virtually impossible to compile a truly complete list of ski resorts of the world. Any hillock which gets the occasional snowflake is skiable. Hampstead Heath is skied from time to time. The following list of resorts has been chosen as a reasonable cross-section of what each country has to offer. Standards vary enormously; what would be a modest resort in Switzerland or Utah might be regarded as highly sophisticated in Turkey or South Africa. Many very good resorts are not in the list—there is simply not the space to cover even quite high standard villages in some European countries and North America.

After the name of the resort you will find the name of the country. This is usually followed by the area in which the resort lies. The final name is that of the main gateway city, particularly for foreigners. In most instances this is an international airport but, in the case of Austria, for example, where the main gateway is usually Munich, it is likely to be the biggest railhead.

The symbols are as follows:

△ for the quality of skiing. One △ basic, △△△△△ superb.

★ for the expense of the resort. ★ cheap, ★★★★★ expensive.

The comparisons are purely local; a dear Spanish resort would doubtless be regarded as a cheap village in Switzerland.

♈ ⑤ For the quality of the *après-ski*. Anything below ③ is pretty basic. ⑤ will mean a discothèque or two. ⑥ – ⑦ means night clubs, too. Above that you might find casinos.

ABETONE, Italy (Appenines); Pisa
△△△ ★★★ ♈ ⑥ Good snow and sunshine record. Quiet weekdays, can be crowded weekends.

ADELBODEN, Switzerland (Bernese Oberland); Zürich (177km)
△△△ ★★★★★ ♈ ⑦ Light-hearted Swiss resort. Pretty village. Good

beginner/intermediate skiing.

AGRIOLEFKES, Greece; Athens

△ ★★ ⟁③ Two ski lifts and reasonable skiing.

ALPBACH, Austria (Tyrol: Wildschönau); Innsbruck

△△△ ★★★⟁⑤ Small, friendly, beginners' favourite. Very attractive village with some night life. Intermediate skiing on top runs.

ALPE D'HUEZ, France (Isère); Grenoble (62km)

△△△△ ★★★★⟁⑥ Very French resort. Popular Grenoble commuter centre. Big ski school. Good sunshine record.

ALPENTHAL, U.S.A. (Washington); Seattle (75km)

△△△ ★★★⟁④ Several surrounding resorts add to good basic skiing.

ALPINE MEADOWS, U.S.A. (California); Reno (64km)

△△△ ★★★⟁⑤ Good intermediate resort, 2,000 acres of skiing.

ALTA, U.S.A. (Utah); Salt Lake City (53km)

△△△ ★★★⟁⑥ Excellent snow record Nov.–May season. Powder resort. Popular with young people.

ALTO CAMPOO, Spain (Cantabria); Santanda (96km)

△△ ★★★⟁③ Wide unwooded intermediate runs. Accommodation mainly at old town of Reinosa.

ALYESKA (MT) U.S.A. (Alaska); Anchorage (64km)

△△ ★★★★⟁③ Unfettered skiing. 19km glacier run. Most runs intermediate. Basic resort but fully equipped.

ANDERMATT, Switzerland (Central); Zürich (72km)

△△△ ★★★⟁⑥ Family centre with reliable snow. But not a resort for beginners.

ANDORRA, see Soldeu and Grau Roig

ANZERE, Switzerland (Valais); Geneva (129km)

△△△ ★★★★⟁⑥ Sophisticated small resort. Close to Crans–Montana complex.

APEX ALPINE, Canada (British Columbia); Vancouver

△△ ★★★⟁② Small resort in Okanagan complex. Main après-ski in Peniction, a one-hour drive.

ARABBA, Italy (Dolomites); Ponte Gardea

△△ ★★⟁④ Small but growing resort with surprisingly good skiing. Unsophisticated après-ski.

ARCS (LES), France (Savoie); Chambery

△△△ ★★★⟁⑤ New resort. Good lift system. Centre of ski évolutif. Popular package tours ex-U.K.

AROSA, Switzerland (Grisons); Zürich (150km)

△△△△ ★★★★⟁⑥ Good lift system and extensive network of multi-grade runs. Friendly resort, active night life.

ASARIGAWA WHITE VALLEY, Japan (Hokkaido); Otaru

△△ ★★★★ ⍥ ③ Smallish but popular.

ASPEN, U.S.A. (Colorado); Denver (319km)

△△△△△ ★★★★ ⍥ ⑦ One of the world's best resorts. Superb varied skiing at Aspen, Aspen Mountain, Highlands and Snowmass. Own airport. Reliable snow.

AVORIAZ, France (Haute Savoie); Geneva

△△△△ ★★★★ ⍥ ⑤ Jet-set new resort. Big ski area linked to Switzerland.

AX-LES-THERMES, France (Pyrénées); Toulouse

△△ ★★ ⍥ ⑤ Simple resort, popular with young people.

BAD GASTEIN, Austria (Salzburgerland); Salzburg.

△△△ ★★★★ ⍥ ⑤ Big spa town, reasonable skiing intermediate upwards. Sophisticated night life.

BAD REICHENHALL, Germany (Bavaria); Salzburg

△△ ★★★ ⍥ ⑤ Limited but pleasant skiing from low-lying spa. Lots of town activity. Uncertain snow.

BAQUEIRA BERET, Spain (Pyrénées); Toulouse (France) (180km)

△△△ ★★★ ⍥ ④ Varied runs, resort very popular with French. Avalanche problems make some road access difficult.

BARILOCHE, Argentina; Cordoba

△△△ ★★★★ ⍥ ④ Spectacular scenery and well-served runs.

BEAR VALLEY, U.S.A. (California); Sacramento (193km)

△△△ ★★★ ⍥ ⑥ Long snow season. Ski touring. Indoor 'bubble'. Videotape ski clinic.

BERCHTESGADEN, Germany (Bavaria); Salzburg

△△△ ★★★★ ⍥ ⑥ Basic downhill but very good ski touring centre. Large town. Lots going on.

BIG WHITE, Canada (British Columbia); Vancouver

△△△ ★★★ ⍥ ③ Good open slopes on very high terrain. Helicopter skiing.

BLED, Yugoslavia (Karavanka); Ljubljana

△△△ ★★ ⍥ ⑦ Town resort by lake. Thermal swimming pools. Other areas nearby.

BOLTON VALLEY, U.S.A. (Vermont); Burlington (29km)

△△△ ★★★ ⍥ ④ Comfortable New England resort. Night skiing. Touring.

BORMIO, Italy (Trentino); Bolzano

△△△△ ★★★ ⍥ ⑥ Runs of all standards, superb ski lift system.

Reliable snow. Summer skiing.

BOROVETS, Bulgaria (Rila); Sofia

△ ★★ ꝩ ③ Good skiing but limited lifts. Long runs. Original Bulgarian ski centre.

BOURG ST MAURICE, France (Savoie); Chambery

△△ ★★★ ꝩ ④ Base station Isère Valley. Good access other areas. *See* Les Arcs.

BRAND, Austria (Vorarlberg); Bludenz (10km)

△△△ ★★ ꝩ ⑤ Good lift system. Exceptional scenery. Very popular with British. Close to Switzerland.

BRECKENRIDGE, U.S.A. (Colorado); Denver (138km)

△△△ ★★★ ꝩ ⑤ Good intermediate resort. Some testing runs. 3,610m summit.

BROMLEY MOUNTAIN, U.S.A. (Vermont); Albany (103km)

△△△ ★★★ ꝩ ⑤ Medium-sized GLM Centre. Popular with families. Good facilities for children.

BROMONT, Canada (Quebec); Montreal

△△△ ★★★★ ꝩ ⑤ Bromont is the nearest to Montreal of half a dozen resorts on Quebec/Vermont border. Jay Peak is on U.S. side.

BULLER (MT), Australia (Victoria); Melbourne (238km)

△△△ ★★★ ꝩ ④ Large resort by local standards. Good skiing but snow can be unreliable. Crowded at weekends but quiet during week.

BURSA, Turkey; Istanbul

△△ ★★★ ꝩ ③ Simple weekend skiing at Mt Uludug.

CAIRNGORMS, Great Britain (Inverness-shire); Inverness (56km)

△△ ★★ ꝩ ⑥ Prime Scottish resort. Late snow. Hearty *après-ski*.

CAMP FORTUNE, Canada (Quebec); Ottawa

△△△ ★★★★ ꝩ ⑥ Four good resorts in area west of Ottawa— Vorlage, Edelweiss, Mt Ste.-Marie and Camp Fortune.

CANDANCHU, Spain (Pyrénées); Zaragoza (180km)

△△△ ★★★ ꝩ ⑤ Modern resort. Broad open skiing. Very popular with French. Best access via Pau airport (France).

CANNON MOUNTAIN, U.S.A. (New Hampshire); Franconia (5km)

△△ ★★★ ꝩ ⑤ Modest resort with good spring skiing.

CARROZ D'ARACHES, France (Haute Savoie); Cluses

△△ ★★ ꝩ ⑤ Simple resort. Ski touring.

CEDARS, Lebanon; Beirut (136km)

△△△ ★★★★ ꝩ ⑤ Only two hours' drive from Beirut. Huge bowl of lofty ski terrain.

CERLER, Spain (Pyrénées); Zaragoza (228km)

△△ ★★★ ♈︎ ③ New resort with varied runs in protected valley. Good for intermediate and better skiers.

CERVINIA, Italy (Aosta); Turin
△△△△△ ★★★★ ♈︎ ⑧ One of Italy's top resorts. Excellent spring snow. Powder at times. Active night life.

CHAMONIX, France (Haute Savoie); Annécy
△△△△△ ★★★★★ ♈︎ ⑧ Superb French resort. Extensive skiing. Summer runs. Fashionable. For the better skier.

CHAMPÉRY, Switzerland (Vaud); Geneva (97km)
△△△△ ★★★ ♈︎ Small extensive ski runs. Links with Avoriaz (France). Good for intermediates.

CHAMROUSSE, France (Isère); Grenoble
△△△△ ★★★★ ♈︎ Residential resort. Relaxed atmosphere. Cross-country centre.

CHÂTEAU D'OEX, Switzerland (Vaud); Geneva
△△ ★★★ ♈︎ ④ Quiet resort, alpine charm. Adjacent bigger more extensive skiing. Horse riding.

CLUSAZ, France (Alpes du Nord); Annécy
△△△ ★★★ ♈︎ ⑥ Commuter resort for Annécy. Airport. Active night life. Extensive skiing.

CORTINA, Italy (Dolomites); Bolzano
△△△△ ★★★★ ♈︎ ⑥ Big resort, one time Olympic Centre. Fashionable. Several good ski areas.

CORVARA, Italy (Dolomites); Ponte Gardena
△△ ★★★ ♈︎ ⑤ Ample skiing, thanks to ski links with nearby areas. Small but popular.

COURCHEVEL, France (Savoie); Lyon
△△△△ ★★★★ ♈︎ ⑦ Big newish resort with some of best European skiing. Communicating lift systems to other resorts. Active night life.

COURMAYEUR, Italy (Mont Blanc); Aosta
△△△△ ★★★★ ♈︎ ⑤ Good skier's resort. Pleasant village close to France.

CRANS-MONTANA, Switzerland (Valais); Geneva (129km)
△△△△ ★★★★ ♈︎ ⑦ Excellent skiing spoiled only by uncertain snow. Superb weather.

DALSETER, Norway, Vinstra (36km)
△△ ★★★ ♈︎ ③ Touring centre of exceptional beauty. Limited downhill.

DAVOS, Switzerland (Grisons); Zürich (153km)
△△△△ ★★★★★ ♈︎ ⑧ One of world's best ski areas. Big town. Recommended to good skiers. Full range ski and *après-ski* facilities.

DIZIN, Iran (Alborz); Tehran

△△△ (*projected*) New resort now being built. Promises to be the best in the region.

ENGELBERG, Switzerland (Bernese-Oberland); Zürich (80km)

△△△ ★★★ ⊤ ⑥ Ancient village with charm and good skiing. Some testing runs.

FAKRA, Lebanon, Beirut

△△△ (*planned*) Will be Lebanon's prestige resort, considerably larger than others.

FALLS CREEK, Australia (Victoria); Melbourne (370km)

△△ ★★★ ⊤ ② Developing area whose distance from Melbourne makes it less crowded than Mt Hotham.

FARAYA, Lebanon, Beirut

△△△ ★★★ ⊤ ⑤ Purpose-built resort, crowded at weekends. Top station 2,600m.

FARELLONES, Chile (Andes); Santiago

△△△ ★★★ ⊤ ③ Well equipped, reliable snow.

FEFOR, Norway (Gudbransdal); Vinstra

△△ ★★★ ⊤ ③ Wide variety of well marked ski trails through lakeside forests.

FIEBERBRUNN, Austria (Kitzbüheler Alpen); Kitzbühel

△△ ★★ ⊤ ⑤ Attractive ambience, close Kitzbühel ski circus, reliable snow. Ideal for beginners and intermediates.

FLAINE, France (Haute Savoie); Cluses

△△△ ★★★★ ⊤ ④ Modern resort. Superb lift system. Snow making equipment. Interesting architecture.

FLIMS, Switzerland (Grisons); Zürich (145km)

△△△ ★★★★ ⊤ ⑤ Attractive resort in wooded area. Mainly villa/apartment accommodation. Extensive skiing.

FONT-ROMFU, France (Pyrénées); Perpignan

△△△ ★★★ ⊤ ⑥ Mainly residential resort, big ski school. Cinema.

FORMIGAL, Spain (Pyrénées); Zaragoza (168km)

△△△ ★★★ ⊤ ⑤ Modern development in open, sunny, sometimes windy, area. Extensive skiing in well-designed system.

FTEROLAKA, Greece; Athens

△△ ★★ ⊤ ② Three chairlifts giving access to enjoyable slopes.

GARGELLEN, Austria (Montafon (Vorarlberg)); Landeck

△△ ★★ ⊤ ⑤ Small, charming, friendly forest resort. Popular. Good for families. Limited skiing with wide slopes for novices and some difficult runs for experts. Good off-*piste* skiing and ski touring.

GARIBALDI, Canada (Rockies); Vancouver (113km)
△△△△ **** ♈⑤ Huge ski area with lots of powder runs. Longest
vertical drop in N. America. Excellent ski school. Summer skiing.
GARMISCH-PARTENKIRCHEN, Germany (Bavaria); Munich
△△△△ **** ♈⑧ Large resort town. Considerable range of runs.
Crowded at weekends. Germany's premier resort.
GASCHURN-PARTENEN, Austria (Montafon (Vorarlberg)); Landeck
△△ ** ♈④ Small sister villages with Gaschurn the larger and prettier.
Reliable snow. Varied skiing. Two main skiing areas. Easy access to
other resorts. Entrypoint for ski touring.
GEILO, Norway (Hardanger); Oslo (240km)
△△△ *** ♈⑥ Downhill resort with mainly intermediate short runs.
Cheerful atmosphere.
GEORGIAN BAY, Canada (Ontario); Toronto
△△△△ **** ♈⑥ At least eight quality resorts around the bay of
Lake Huron. Active night life in area.
GETS, France (Haute Savoie); Annemasse
△△ *** ♈⑤ Close to Geneva Airport, popular active resort.
GLENCOE, Great Britain (West Scottish Highlands); Tyndrum
(56km)
△△ ** ♈② Basic resort but snow more reliable than Scots norm.
GLENSHEE, Great Britain (Perthshire); Aberdeen (55km)
△△ ** ♈④ Scattered accommodation around growing resort. Long
season, but snow can be unreliable.
GRAU ROIG, Andorra (Pyrénées); Barcelona
△△ ** ♈⑥ Higher standard of runs than at nearby Soldeu. Good off-
piste opportunities.
GRINDELWALD, Switzerland (Bernese-Oberland); Zürich (177km)
△△△△ **** ♈⑥ Delightful resort, ideal for families. Good downhill and touring.
GROUSE MOUNTAIN, Canada (Rockies); Vancouver (10km)
△△△ *** ♈⑤ On Vancouver's doorstep. Very good for beginners.
Spectacular views.
GSTAAD, Switzerland (Vaud); Geneva
△△△△ ***** ♈⑦ Old, established, expensive glamour resort with
very good skiing for all standards. Centre for the villa-owning jet set.
GULMARG, India (Kashmir); Srinagar
△△△ *** ♈② Himalayan skiing with magnificent views. Good snow
Dec.–March. Very high (2,700m).

HAJI UMRAN, Iraq (Kurdistan); Baghdad
△ ★★ ⍦ ① Exotic location makes some take the journey. Closest big town is Kirkuk (161km).

HAPPO-ONE, Japan (Chubu); Tokyo
△△△△ ★★★★ ⍦ ⑤ Recommended for better skiers. Very steep runs.

HARRACHOV, Czechoslovakia (Giant Mountains); Prague (145km)
△△△ ★★ ⍦ ④ Long established. Ski jumping centre. Bob-sleigh runs.

HEAVENLY VALLEY, U.S.A. (California); Reno (90km)
△△△△ ★★★★ ⍦ ⑦ Sophisticated big resort, extensive facilities. Gaming.

HEMSEDAHL, Norway; Oslo (230km)
△△△ ★★★ ⍦ ④ All round resort with good downhill and touring facilities. Spectacular scenery.

HIDDEN VALLEY, Canada (Ontario); Toronto
△△△ ★★★ ⍦ ⑤ One of the best of the resorts near Lake Vernon.

HINDELANG, Germany (Allgäu); Munich
△△ ★★★★ ⍦ ⑤ Simple resort twinned with spa town of Oberdorf.

HINTERGLEMM, Austria (Pinzgau); Salzburg
△△ ★★ ⍦ ⑤ Twin resort of Saalbach. Simple family atmosphere, but better than average après-ski and access to good skiing.

HINTERTUX, Austria (Zillertal; Tyrol); Innsbruck
△△△ ★★ ⍦ ④ Base resort for Tuxer Lift complex, gateway for high ski touring. Natural thermal springs. Long season, including local summer glacier skiing. Simple après-ski. Suitable for keen, medium-standard skiers.

HOTHAM (MT), Australia (Victoria); Melbourne (370km)
△△ ★★★ ⍦ ② Expanding, small resort with acceptable all round skiing.

ILESUY, Spain (Pyrénées); Barcelona (258km)
△△ ★★★ ⍦ ③ Broad, open, sunshine skiing in Baixens valley.

ISCHGL, Austria (Paznautal, Tyrol); St Anton
△△△ ★★★ ⍦ ⑥ Recently developed and improved ski resort. Traditional-style village, cable car access to main ski areas, for touring enthusiasts and medium standard skiers.

JACKSON HOLE, U.S.A. (Wyoming); Salt Lake City (434km)
△△△ ★★★ ⍦ ⑤ All round resort, easy going. Good for reliable snow. Long runs.

KANDERSTEG, Switzerland (Bernese-Oberland); Zürich (233km)
△△△ ★★★ ⍦ ⑤ Charming little village with old-world Swiss attraction. Good skiing, particularly for beginners and intermediates.

KAPRUN, Austria (Pinzgau); Salzburg

△△ ★★★ ⟙ ⑤   Very high, summer glacier skiing. Resort for serious skiers.

KEYSTONE, U.S.A. (Colorado); Denver (116km)
△△△ ★★★ ⟙ ⑤   Developing new area particularly good for middle standard skiers.

KILLINGTON, U.S.A. (Vermont); Boston (241km)
△△△ ★★★★ ⟙ ⑥   Popular resort, ample beginner facilities and some expert runs. World's longest ski lift (5·6km).

KINGSFIELD, U.S.A. (Maine); Boston
△△△ ★★★ ⟙ ⑥   Rapidly growing home of sugarloaf skiing. Superbly planned slopes giving good long runs.

KIRKWOOD, U.S.A. (California); Reno (113km)
△△ ★★ ⟙ ④   Ski touring centre. Good intermediate downhill resort.

KITANOMINE KOKUSETSU, Japan (Hokkaido); Furano
△△ ★★★★ ⟙ ③   Basic northern resort.

KITZBÜHEL, Austria (Tyrol); Innsbruck
△△△△△ ★★★★ ⟙ ⑧   Large historic town with international character. Variety of skiing for all levels, all types of après-ski. One of the top Austrian resorts.

KLOSTERS, Switzerland (Grisons); Zürich (161km)
△△△△ ★★★★ ⟙ ⑦   Close to Davos, with access to its skiing. Pretty village, fashionable but intimate. Good skiing.

KRANJSKA GORA, Yugoslavia (Julian Alps); Ljubljana
△△ ★★ ⟙ ④   Popular northern Yugoslav village. Ski jumping.

KÜHTAI, Austria (Oetztal); Innsbruck
△△△ ★★★ ⟙ ⑤   Favoured high resort retaining old world gentility. Ski touring centre. Reliable snow.

KUROHIME, Japan (Chudu); Tokyo
△△ ★★★ ⟙ ④   Less crowded than most Japanese resorts. Good intermediate shirakaba run.

LAKE LOUISE, Canada (Rockies); Calgary
△△△ ★★★ ⟙ ⑤   Self-contained compact resort with good atmosphere. Variety of runs at all standards. Reliable snow.

LAKLOUK, Lebanon; Beirut (70km)
△ ★★★ ⟙ ③   Small resort with limited capacity. Relaxed fun skiing.

LA MOLINA, Spain (Pyrénées); Barcelona (155km)
△△△ ★★★ ⟙ ⑤   Extensive skiing of various standards; one Olympic run. One of Spain's bigger resorts, and linked to Super Molina.

LA MONGIE, France (Pyrénées); Tarbes
△△△ ★★★ ⟙ ④   Ski touring centre. Largest ski school in West

Pyrénées.

LANERSBACH, Austria (Zillertal, Tyrol); Innsbruck
△ ★★ ⅋ ② Small quiet resort for beginners and moderate skiers.

LA PARVA, Chile (Andes); Santiago
△△△ ★★★ ⅋ ④ High resort with long runs and good snow.

LA PLAGNE, France (Savoie); Chambéry
△△△△ ★★★ ⅋ ⑤ Bigger new resort. Good intermediate skiing. Extensive lift system.

LECH AM ARLBERG, Austria (Vorarlberg); Landeck
△△△△ ★★★ ⅋ ⑥ Small, popular and sometimes crowded village resort. High and sunny, extensive well-planned ski area. Suitable for families and all grades of skiers.

LE MONT DORE, France (Puy de Dome); Clermont-Ferrand
△△ ★★★ ⅋ ⑤ Small resort but ample accommodation and good night life. Casino.

LENK, Switzerland (Bernese-Oberland); Geneva (193km)
△△△ ★★★ ⅋ ⑥ Pretty village with broad range of skiing and some touring.

LENZERHEIDE, Switzerland (Grisons); Zürich
△△△ ★★★ ⅋ ④ Nice resort with lots of woodland, car useful. Ample skiing, not so ample après-ski.

LERMOOS, Austria (Lecthaler Alpen, Tyrol); Garmisch
△△△ ★★ ⅋ ⑤ Main road village. For skiers up to medium level. Excursions Innsbruck/Zugspitze Mountain/Garmisch-Partenkirchen. Ski jumping. Casual après-ski.

LES DEUX ALPES, France (Isère); Grenoble
△△△△ ★★★ ⅋ ⑦ One of the bigger new resorts. Excellent lift system. Linked runs. Young atmosphere.

LES DIABLERETS, Switzerland (Vaud); Geneva (121km)
△△△ ★★★ ⅋ ⑤ Small village below huge mountains. Glacier skiing. Late season is best.

LES MARECOTTES, Switzerland (Valais); Geneva (80km)
△△ ★★★ ⅋ ④ Simple little resort but long runs. Small ski school.

LES MENUIRES, France (Savoie); Grenoble
△△△ ★★★ ⅋ ⑤ New station. Communicating trails to other resorts. Ski touring.

LES ROUSSES, France (Jura); Morez
△△△ ★★ ⅋ ④ Residential and commuter resort. Wide range of trails.

LEYSIN, Switzerland (Vaud); Geneva (161km)
△△△ ★★★★ ⅋ ⑤ Sunny skiing, good place for beginners and inter-

mediates. Superb views but lacking a little in atmosphere.

LIENZ, Austria (Ost Tyrol); Klagenfurt
△△ ★★★ ⟨ (7) Big town. Adequate skiing. Modest prices.

LILLEHAMMER, Norway (Gudbransdal); Oslo
△△△ ★★★ ⟨ (5) Pleasant small town beside Lake Mjøsa. Basic downhill facilities, good touring.

LIVIGNO, Italy (Trentino); Bormio (40km)
△△△ ★★★ ⟨ (5) Duty free area. Long, strung-out valley. Good resort
for intermediates.

LOON MT, U.S.A. (New Hampshire); Littleton (26km)
△△ ★★★★ ⟨ (4) Commuter resort. 115 acres of ski terrain.

LOS COTOS PASS, Spain (Central); Madrid (70km)
△△△ ★★★ ⟨ (4) Skiing in two main areas in sheltered valley.

LOVELAND (Basin and Valley), U.S.A. (Colorado); Denver (90km)
△△△ ★★★ ⟨ (5) Commuter resort for Denver. Very high (3,292m at
base).

MACUGNAGA, Italy (Piedmont); Milan
△△△ ★★ ⟨ (5) Good skiing; intermediate's resort. Inexpensive.
Popular with British skiers.

MADESIMO, Italy (Como); Milan (145km)
△△△ ★★★ ⟨ (6) Shares mountain range with St Moritz (no link).
Reliable snow. Compact lift system. Resort for better skiers.

MALBUN, Liechtenstein (Vaduz); Zürich (9km)
△△ ★★ ⟨ (4) Small village in independent state. Beginner's resort.
Good quiet family centre.

MALLNITZ, Austria (Carinthia); Salzburg
△△ ★★ ⟨ (5) Simple, usually uncrowded ski touring possibilities.
Favoured Dutch package resort.

MARMOT BASIN, Canada (Rockies); Calgary
△△△ ★★★★ ⟨ (5) One of Rockies' best ski centres. Superb extensive
runs of various standards.

MASELLA, Spain (Pyrénées); Barcelona (150km)
△△ ★★ ⟨ (3) Forest skiing (unusual in Spain) with open slopes at top.
Good, simple lift system.

MATROOSBERG, South Africa (Cape Province); Cape Town
△△ ★★★ ⟨ (2) Basic little fun resort. A healthy drive from Cape Town.
Mainly club skiing.

MAUNA KEA, U.S.A. (Hawaii); Hilo
△ ★★★★ ⟨ (2) Skiing for the adventurous. No lifts; trucks used.
4,205m. Not recommended for heart patients. Good snow in January.

MAYRHOFEN, Austria (Zillertal); Innsbruck
△△△ ★★ ⛄ ⑥   Bustling and popular, with good, hearty *après-ski.*
Interesting skiing on Ahorn and Penken slopes. Crowded lifts at peak
times.

MEGÈVE, France (Haute Savoie); Geneva
△△△△△ ★★★★★ ⛄ ⑧   Big French resort. Very high standard of
skiing. Ski touring. Casino. Busy night life.

MÉRIBEL, France (Savoie); Moutiers
△△△ ★★★ ⛄ ⑤   Growing modern resort. Links with Courchevel.
Wooded runs. Good for families.

META BIEF, France (Doubs); Vallorbe (Switzerland)
△△△ ★★★ ⛄ ④   Small commuter resort. Interesting skiing. Popular at
weekends.

METSOVON, Greece; Athens
△ ★★ ⛄ ②   One small lift for very basic skiing. Closed Wednesdays.

MITTENWALD, Germany (Bavaria); Munich
△△△ ★★★★ ⛄ ④   Pretty little old village, pleasant simple skiing.

MONTGENÈVRE, France (Haute Alpes); Briancon (22km)
△△△ ★★★ ⛄ ⑤   Small, good lift system. Intermediate skiing. Close to
Italian border.

MONT SAINTE-ANNE, Canada (Québec); Québec
△△△ ★★★★ ⛄ ⑤   Extensive skiing within easy reach of Québec. World
Cup resort. Runs of all standards.

MONT TREMBLANT, Canada (Québec); Montreal
△△△ ★★★ ⛄ ⑥   Lots of skiing on mountain and in surrounding area.
Good accommodation. French atmosphere.

MT BACHELOR, U.S.A. (Oregon); Portland (253km)
△△△ ★★★★ ⛄ ⑤   U.S. ski team training centre. Short runs. Good
deep snow.

MT CHOPOK, Czechoslovakia (Low Tatras); Prague
△△△ ★★ ⛄ ⑤   Varied skiing, active rural-style night life.

MT COOK, New Zealand (Southern Alps); Christchurch
△△△△ ★★★★ ⛄ ④   Extensive, and expensive, skiing. Aircraft rental
possible to ski glacier.

MT CORONET, New Zealand (Southern Alps); Christchurch
△△△ ★★★ ⛄ ⑤   Extensively developed. Good skiing, friendly
atmosphere.

MT EGMONT, New Zealand (North Island); Auckland
△△△ ★★★ ⛄ ③   Well developed resort, can be crowded at peak
season.

MT RUAPEHU, New Zealand (North Island); Auckland
△△△ ★★★ ♀ ④ Slopes dominated by club skiing. Good downhill runs.

MT SNOW, U.S.A. (Vermont); New York (351km)
△△△△ ★★★★ ♀ ⑥ Popular weekend centre. Big ski school.

MÜRREN, Switzerland (Bernese-Oberland); Zürich (144km)
△△△ ★★★★ ♀ ⑥ Delightful resort with pleasant village and good skiing in spectacular scenery.

MYOKO KOGEN, Japan (Chubu); Tokyo
△△△△ ★★★★ ♀ ④ Large ski area, good rail link with Tokyo. Longish runs.

NAEBA, Japan (Joshn-etsu); Tokyo
△△△ ★★★★ ♀ ⑤ Popular resort, close to Tokyo. Good lifts. Very crowded at weekends.

NASU-YUMOTO, Japan (Nikko); Tokyo (161km)
△△ ★★★★ ♀ ③ Beginner's playground. Ski touring.

NAUDERS, Austria (Komperdell); Landeck
△ ★★★ ♀ ④ Compact resort. Very pretty region. Limited skiing.

NAVACERRADA PASS, Spain (Central); Madrid (62km)
△△ ★★★ ♀ ④ High skiing with pine forests at lower levels. Bad weather sometimes closes some lifts.

NIEDERAU, Austria (Wildschonau); Wörgl
△△ ★★★ ♀ ④ Small village. Short runs but well served. Good practice slopes, with better skiing up top.

NORDSETER, Norway (Gubransdal); Oslo
△△ ★★★ ♀ ③ Sleepy little resort with gentle touring trails. Nursery downhill.

NOREFJELL, Norway (Buskerud); Oslo
△△△ ★★★★ ♀ ⑤ One of Norway's prime downhill areas, good touring. Limited accommodation.

NORQUAY, Canada (Rockies); Calgary
△△ ★★★ ♀ ③ Small resort close to Banff. Mostly gentle skiing but one or two very testing runs.

NORTH STAR, Canada (British Columbia); Kimberley
△△ ★★★ ♀ ④ Deep snow resort. Good runs, of varying standards, through trees.

NORTHSTAR, U.S.A. (California); Reno (63km)
△△△ ★★★ ♀ ④ Good intermediate and some expert skiing. Touring centre.

NURIA, Spain (Pyrénées); Barcelona (135km)

△ ★★ ♈ ②   Simple mountain refuge station. Superb lake scenery nearby.

OBERGURGL, Austria (Oetztal); Innsbruck

△△△ ★★★ ♈ ⑥   Three linked resorts: Ober, Unter and Hochgurgl. High villages, long season multi-grade skiing.

OBERSTDORF, Germany (Allgau); Munich

△△△ ★★★★ ♈ ⑥   Large spa resort. Good intermediate skiing. Spectacular jumping.

ORTISEI, Italy (Val Gardena); Fortezza

△△ ★★★ ♈ ⑤   Close to Austrian border. Popular family resort. Friendly atmosphere.

OSLO, Norway

△△ ★★★★ ♈ ⑥   Various downhill runs around city. Good cross-country.

OUKAI-MEDAN, Morocco (Atlas); Marrakech

△△△ ★★★ ♈ ③   Surprisingly good sunshine skiing.

PAJARES PASS, Spain (Cantabria); Asturias (100km)

△ ★★ ♈ ③   Quiet little centre with its own parador. Unhurried skiing.

PAMPOROVO, Bulgaria (Rhodopes Mountains); Sofia (241km)

△△△ ★★ ♈ ⑤   Modern, good lift system. Adjacent Greek border.

PANTICOSA, Spain (Pyrénées); Zaragoza (154km)

△△ ★★ ♈ ④   Charming old village with good sheltered skiing on broad slopes. Very good for intermediates.

PARK CITY, U.S.A. (Utah); Salt Lake City (56km)

△△△ ★★★ ♈ ④   Salt Lake commuter ski resort. Broad *pistes*. Mining village atmosphere. Odd drink laws. Big ski school.

PERISHER, Australia (N.S.W.); Sydney (520km)

△△△ ★★★ ♈ ⑤   Reliable snow and good lift system (mainly tows). Excellent for families. Good Austrian ski school. Skiing, too, at nearby Smiggins Hole.

PINILLA, Spain (Central); Madrid (120km)

△△ ★★★ ♈ ③   Rapidly growing area offering open, un-testing skiing. An easy drive from Madrid.

POIANA BRASOV, Romania (Carpathians); Brasov (16km)

△△ ★★ ♈ ④   Good lift system. Floodlit skiing.

PONTRESINA, Switzerland (Grisons); Zürich (201km)

△△△ ★★★★ ♈ ⑥   Adjacent St Moritz. Picturesque village centre. Dispersed skiing. Good late snow.

PORTILLO, Chile (Andes); Santiago

△△△ ★★★★ ♈ ⑤   June-September resort. Very popular with Americans. Mainly intermediate runs.

PRA-LOUP, France (Haute Provence); Gap

△△△ ★★★ ⵏ ⑤ Intermediate resort. Extensive residential accommodation. Large ski area.

PURGATORY, U.S.A. (Colorado); Durango (40km)

△△ ★★★ ⵏ ⑤ Rapidly improving new resort. Ski jumping.

ROTTACH, Germany (Bavaria); Munich

△△ ★★★ ⵏ ③ Lakeside village with simple relaxed skiing.

SAALBACH, Austria (Pinzgau); Salzburg

△△△ ★★★ ⵏ ⑥ Part of extensive sport region complex. Above average *après-ski*.

SAAS-FEE, Switzerland (Valais); Geneva (177km)

△△△ ★★★★ ⵏ ⑥ Start of *haute route*. Compact village, wooden houses, long snow season. Informal night life.

ST ANTON, Austria (Arlberg); Landeck

△△△△△ ★★★★ ⵏ ⑨ One of the world's top ski areas. Famous ski school. Recommended for experts. Arlberg circuit gives unlimited skiing. Can get crowded.

ST CERGUE, Switzerland (Vaud); Geneva (64km)

△△ ★★★ ⵏ ④ Small sunny Jura village. Good view of Lake Geneva. Good for beginners.

ST GERVAIS, France (Haute Savoie); Geneva

△△△ ★★★★ ⵏ ⑧ Bustling resort with access to other areas. Active night life.

ST JAKOB, Austria (Ost Tyrol); Lienz

△△△ ★★ ⵏ ④ Rapidly developing area close to Italian border. Good snow record. Wide treeless runs.

ST MORITZ, Switzerland (Grisons); Zürich (201km)

△△△△ ★★★★★ ⵏ ⑩ Large, luxurious, fashionable, expensive. Superb skiing. Good sunshine.

SAMOËNS, France (Haute Savoie); Geneva

△△ ★★★ ⵏ ⑤ Small resort, good reasonable accommodation.

SANI PASS, South Africa (Drakensberg); Durban

△△ ★★★ ⵏ ③ Developing area in mountains bordering Lesotho.

SAN ISIDRO, Spain (Cantabria); Asturias (70km)

△ ★★ ⵏ ③ Old village below simple ski lay-out. Quiet, relaxed resort.

SANTA CATERINA, Italy (Trentino); Bormio (8km)

△△ ★★ ⵏ ⑤ Small, delightful resort. Good snow. Close to bustling Bormio.

SAN VALENTINO, Italy (Dolomites); Landeck (Austria)

△△ ★★ ♈③ By two lakes (skating). Small village. Austrian atmosphere.

SAUZE D'OULX, Italy (Piedmont); Turin

△△△ ★★★ ♈⑥ Bustling resort, close to Turin. Ample skiing for the better intermediate.

SAVOGNIN, Switzerland (Grisons); Munich (145km)

△△ ★★★ ♈⑤ Smallish resort with limited accommodation. Top runs quite high.

SCHLIERSEE, Germany (Bavaria); Munich

△△△ ★★★★ ♈④ Large attractive resort with good nearby skiing.

SCHRUNS, Austria (Vorarlberg); Montafon

△△△ ★★★ ♈⑥ Large spread-out, bustling resort and health centre. Well-planned lift system with projected improvements.

SEEFELD, Austria (Mieminger); Innsbruck

△△△ ★★★★ ♈⑧ Comfortable, pretty resort. Adequate skiing, extensive *après-ski*, swimming, skating, riding, ski touring.

SELVA, Italy (Val Gardena); Ponte Gardena

△△△ ★★★ ♈⑥ Spectacular scenery. Good intermediate skiing. Good sunshine record.

SERFAUS, Austria (Komperdell); Landeck

△△ ★★ ♈⑤ Very pretty village at end of valley. Little traffic. Good sunshine record. Friendly.

SERRA DA ESTRELA, Portugal; Lisbon

△ ★★ ♈② Uncertain snow, very basic facilities.

SERRE-CHEVALIER, France (Haute Alpes); Briançon

△△△ ★★ ♈⑤ Popular French resort with broad range of accommodation and skiing.

SHAHRESTANAK, Iran (Alborz); Tehran

△△ ★★★ ♈② High resort. Rapidly expanding. Close to Tehran.

SHEMSHAK, Iran (Alborz); Tehran

△△ ★★★ ♈② Twin resort with Shahrestanak. Very high, 3,000m at top station.

SHIGA, Japan (Nagano); Tokyo

△△△ ★★★★ ♈⑤ Big resort. Famous for early powder. Good weather record.

SIERRA NEVADA, Spain (Granada); Malaga (160km)

△△△ ★★★★ ♈⑤ Spectacular sunshine skiing close to Mediterranean. Wide clear runs. No trees. Modern purpose-built resort.

SILVER STAR, Canada (British Columbia); Vancouver

△△ ★★★ ♈③ Main entertainment and shopping at nearby Vernon. Good family centre, open skiing on reliable snow.

SJUSJOEN, Norway (Gubransdal); Oslo
△△ ★★★ ϒ ③ Simple touring resort with an away-from-it-all atmosphere.
SKEIKAMPEN, Norway (Gubransdal); Oslo
△△△ ★★★ ϒ ④ Twin resort with Gausdal. Well signposted trails for touring. Some downhill.
SNOWBIRD, U.S.A. (Utah); Salt Lake City (40km)
△△△△ ★★★ ϒ ④ Pedestrian orientated resort. Very good expert ski runs. Powder.
SNOWMASS (see Aspen)
SÖLDA, Italy (Dolomites); Landeck (Austria)
△△ ★★★ ϒ ④ Small, simple village. Basic all-round skiing. Reliable snow.
SÖLDEN, Austria (Oetzal); Innsbruck
△△ ★★★ ϒ ⑥ Linked with Hochsölden. Tree-lined runs but some good high black *pistes*. Good lively *après-ski*.
SOLDEU, Andorra (Pyrénées); Barcelona
△△ ★★★ ϒ ⑥ Intermediate skiing in tiny sovereign duty-free state. *Après-ski* (in Andorra la Vella) 12 miles away.
SÖLL, Austria (Kitzbüheler Alpen); Kitzbühel
△△ ★★ ϒ ④ Close to German border. Small attractive resort. Good skiing some way from village. Off-*piste* opportunities.
ŠPINDLERUV MLÝN, Czechoslovakia (High Tatras); Prague (145km)
△△△ ★★ ϒ ④ Extensive skiing for all standards.
SQUAW VALLEY, U.S.A. (California); Reno (64km)
△△△ ★★★ ϒ ⑦ Large resort with big lift capacity. Flattering skiing.
STARÝ SMOKOVEL, Czechoslovakia (High Tatras); Prague
△△△ ★★ ϒ ⑤ Top Czech resort. Toboganning, cross-country.
STEAMBOAT, U.S.A. (Colorado); Denver (241km)
△△△ ★★★ ϒ ④ Extensive wide run skiing. Well-designed lift system. GLM centre. Billy Kidd (Olympic Gold) is the resort ski director.
STONEHAM, Canada (Québec); Québec
△△ ★★★★ ϒ ⑤ Twin resort with Lac Delage. Good intermediate skiing in trees. Close to Québec.
STOWE, U.S.A. (Vermont); New York (520km)
△△△ ★★★★ ϒ ⑥ One of best known U.S. resorts. Ski touring. Good downhill runs, some very testing.
STRBSKÉ PLESO, Czechoslovakia (High Tatras); Prague

177

△△ ★★ ⓉⓇ ④ Good for beginners and intermediates.

SUGARBUSH VALLEY, U.S.A. (Vermont); Albany (241km)

△△△ ★★★ Ⓣ ⑤ Complete medium-sized resort. Touring trails and rentals. Snow-making equipment.

SUNSHINE, Canada (Rockies); Calgary

△△△ ★★★ Ⓣ ④ Compact ski area with no cars allowed. Main *après-ski* in Banff. Well-planned lift system in attractive setting.

SUN VALLEY, U.S.A. (Idaho); Boise (249km)

△△△△ ★★★★ Ⓣ ⑥ Varied skiing for all levels. Fashionable. Good lift system. Indoor horse-riding.

SUPER BAGNÉRES, France (Pyrénées); Luchon

△△ ★★★ Ⓣ ⑤ Compact but fully-equipped resort. Good lift system. Large ski school.

SUPER-BESSE, France (Puy de Dome); Clermont-Ferrand

△△ ★★★ Ⓣ ⑤ Very close to Clermont-Ferrand. Popular with young people. Ski links with Le Mont Dore.

SUPER DEVOLUY, France (Haute Alpes); Gap

△△ ★★★ Ⓣ ④ Residential resort. Interesting but limited skiing.

SUPER ESPOT, Spain (Pyrénées); Barcelona (270km)

△ ★★★ Ⓣ ③ Sheltered little resort accessible from France, likely to expand rapidly.

TAOS, U.S.A. (New Mexico); Albuquerque (241km)

△△△ ★★★ Ⓣ ④ Alpine-like village atmosphere. Powder skiing through trees. Good expert's resort.

TATRANSKÁ LOMNICA, Czechoslovakia (High Tatras); Prague

△△△ ★★ Ⓣ ④ High standard runs, floodlit slalom.

TEINE OLYMPIA, Japan (Hokkaido); Sapporo

△△△ ★★★★ Ⓣ ⑧ Floodlit skiing.

THREDBO, Australia (N.S.W.); Sydney (518km)

△△△△ ★★★★ Ⓣ ⑥ Best skiing in Australia when snow is good. Excellent steep, challenging, but short, runs. Active night life. Can be very crowded.

THUNDER BAY, Canada (Ontario); Toronto

△△ ★★★ Ⓣ ⑤ Pleasant intermediate skiing with some testing runs here and at Mt Baldy, Mt McKay and Candy Mountains.

TIGNES, France (Savoie); Bourg St Maurice

△△△△ ★★★★★ Ⓣ ⑤ Upper station for Val d'Isère. Good lift system. Superb skiing for higher standards. (*See also* Val d'Isère.)

TROODOS, Cyprus; Nicosia

△ ★★ Ⓣ ② Skiing in Mediterranean sunshine. Simple, fun, diversionary centre. Basic, but lift and ski rental.

UNTERWASSER, Switzerland (St Gallen); Zürich (97km)
△△△ ★★★ ♈ ④ Small resort with few runs but simple unfussy mood.

USTAOSET, Norway (Hallingdal); Bergen
△△△ ★★★ ♈ ③ High touring resort, magnificent scenery. Can be very cold.

VAIL, U.S.A. (Colorado); Denver (161km)
△△△△ ★★★★ ♈ ⑤ Prestige, establishment resort. Perfectly-maintained runs. Famous for the 'Back Bowls' with extensive virgin powder snow.

VAL D'ISÉRE, France (Savoie); Bourg St Maurice
△△△△△ ★★★★★ ♈ ⑥ Europe's best all-round ski centre, but weak on après-ski. Unsurpassed linked ski circus.

VERBIER, Switzerland (Valais); Geneva (145km)
△△△△ ★★★★ ♈ ⑥ Superb open skiing at high altitudes. Lots of sunshine.

VERMION MT, Greece; Athens
△ ★★ ♈ ② Modest skiing in pleasant sunny conditions.

VILLARS, Switzerland (Vaud); Geneva (121km)
△△△ ★★★ ♈ ⑤ Solid Swiss resort with good skiing but which loses its snow early. Popular with families.

VITOSHA, Bulgaria; Sofia (16km)
△ ★★ ♈ ③ Very beautiful. Unsophisticated. Reliable late snow.

VOSS, Norway (Voss); Bergen
△△△△ ★★★★ ♈ ⑤ Main alpine resort of Norway. 24km of downhill runs. Scenic. Friendly village.

WAGRAIN, Austria (Radstadter Tauern); Salzburg
△△△ ★★ ♈ ③ Austria's 'prettiest village'. Home of Anne Marie Proëll. Extensive but rambling ski area.

WENGEN, Switzerland (Bernese-Oberland); Zürich
△△△ ★★★★ ♈ ⑥ No cars. Popular with families. Wide range of runs.

WESTCASTLE, Canada (Rockies); Calgary
△△ ★★★ ♈ ④ Small resort but with some good skiing, particularly for better skiers. Site of 1975 Canadian Winter Games.

WHISTLER (see Garibaldi)

WINTER PARK, U.S.A. (Colorado); Denver (108km)
△△△ ★★★ ♈ ⑤ Close to Denver, popular at weekends. Large ski school.

ZAKOPANE, Poland (High Tatras); Kraków (121km)
△△△ ★★ ♈ ⑥ Premier Polish resort. Very long runs, lots of lifts.

Active night life.

ZAO, Japan (Tohoku); Yamagata

△△△ ★★★★ ¥ ⑤ Village of the Ice Monsters (frozen trees) of Mt Jizo. Long downhill course.

ZATERNICK, Yugoslavia (Karavanka); Bled

△ ★★ ¥ ③ New, simple resort.

ZELL-AM-SEE, Austria (Pinzgau); Salzburg

△△ ★★ ¥ ⑤ Lakeside, broad runs. Excellent for beginners.

ZERMATT, Switzerland (Valais); Geneva (193km)

△△△△ ★★★★★ ¥ ⑦ Best of skiing but not much for beginners. Ski into Italy. Sophisticated night life.

ZUOZ, Switzerland (Grisons); Zürich (201km)

△△ ★★★ ¥ ④ Suburb of St Moritz. Limited skiing. Good centre for seeing area.

ZÜRS, Austria (Arlberg); Landeck

△△△ ★★★★ ¥ ⑥ Fashionable, high quality skiing. Linked with Lech centre for keen and better-off skiers.

APPENDIX 2
National Tourist Offices in Great Britain

AUSTRALIA
Australia Tourist Commission
49 Old Bond Street
London W1X 4PL Tel 01-499 2247/8
AUSTRIA
Austrian National Tourist Office
16 Conduit Street
London W1R 0AL Tel 01-629 0461
BULGARIA
Bulgarian National Tourist Office
126 Regent Street
London W1R 5FE Tel 01-437 2611/2
CANADA
Canadian Government Travel Bureau
PO Box 9, Canada House
Trafalgar Square
London SW1Y 5DR Tel 01-930 0731
CYPRUS
Cyprus Tourist Centre
213 Regent Street
London W1R 8DA Tel 01-734 9822
CZECHOSLOVAKIA
Czechoslovak Travel Bureau
17–18 Old Bond Street
London W1X 3DA Tel 01-629 6058/9
FINLAND
Finnish Tourist Board
Finland House
56 Haymarket
London SW1Y 4RN Tel 01-839 4048

FRANCE
French Government Tourist Office
178 Piccadilly
London W1V 0AL Tel 01-493 3171
GERMANY
German Tourist Information Bureau
61 Conduit Street
London W1R 0EN Tel 01-734 2600
GREECE
National Tourist Organisation of Greece
195–197 Regent Street
London W1R 8DL Tel 01-734 5997
INDIA
Government of India Tourist Office
21 New Bond Street
London W1Y 0DY Tel 01-493 0769
IRAN
Iran National Tourist Organisation
16 Princes Gate
London SW7 1PX Tel 01-584 8101
ITALY
Italian State Tourist Office (ENIT)
201 Regent Street
London W1R 8AY Tel 01-734 4631
JAPAN
Japan National Tourist Organisation
167 Regent Street
London W1R 7FD Tel 01-734 9638
LEBANON
Lebanon Tourist and Information Office
90 Piccadilly
London W1 Tel 01-409 2031
MOROCCO
Moroccan National Tourist Office
174 Regent Street
London W1R 6HP Tel 01-437 0073/4
NEW ZEALAND
New Zealand National Tourist Office
New Zealand House, Haymarket
London SW1Y 4TQ Tel 01-930 8422

NORWAY
Norwegian National Tourist Office
20 Pall Mall
London SW1Y 5NE Tel 01-839 6255
POLAND
Polish Travel Office 'Orbis'
313 Regent Street
London W1R 7PE Tel 01-580 8028
SOUTH AFRICA
South African Tourist Corporation
13 Lower Regent Street
London SW1Y 4LR Tel 01-839 7462/3/4
SPAIN
Spanish National Tourist Office
70 Jermyn Street
London SW1Y 6PD Tel 01-930 8578
SWEDEN
Press & Information Department
The Royal Swedish Embassy
23 North Row
London W1R 2DN Tel 01-499 9500
SWITZERLAND
Swiss National Tourist Office
Swiss Centre, 1 New Coventry Street
London W1V 3HG Tel 01-734 1921
TURKEY
Turkish Tourism & Information Office
49 Conduit Street
London W1R 0EP Tel 01-734 8681/2
USA
United States Travel Service
22 Sackville Street
London W1X 2EA
USSR
Intourist Moscow Limited
292 Regent Street
London W1R 6QL Tel 01-580 4974
YUGOSLAVIA
Yugoslav National Tourist Office
143 Regent Street
London W1R 8AE Tel 01-734 5243

APPENDIX 3
European Summer Skiing

For summer skiing you need glaciers, and there are a number of good areas in Europe for this. It is usually possible to ski only in the morning, and most of the following resorts also have more traditional summer facilities like swimming, golf and tennis.

1. **AUSTRIA**
   Dachstein-Schladming
   Grossglockner
   Hintertux
   Hochgurgl
   Kaprun
   Neustift-Tyrol

2. **FRANCE**
   Alpes d'Heuz
   Les Deux Alpes
   Tignes
   Val d'Isère
   Val Thorens

3. **ITALY**
   Cervinia
   Courmayeur
   Marmolada
   Stelvio/Bormio

4. **SWITZERLAND**
   Andermatt
   Corvatsch-St Moritz
   Crans-Montana
   Engelberg
   Jungfraujoch
   Les Diablerets
   Mürren-Schilthorn
   Pontresina-Dia Volezza
   Saas-Fee
   Zermatt

APPENDIX 4
Ski Club of Great Britain ski testing ratings

The SCGB Tests are recognised by the alpine and other European ski authorities as of a high standard, particularly the Gold and Silver which indicate a skier's competence in all snow conditions.

Running tests and their aims are as follows:

Bronze (3rd) The skier must be able to follow a leader down a fairly easy run at a slow speed; be able to execute controlled and definite turns and stop at any given time.

Silver (2nd) The skier must be able to ski at a steady speed in all snow conditions on- and off-*piste*. He would not be expected to find his own line, but should be able to follow day or weekend tours.

Gold (1st) The skier must be able to recognise different snow conditions and be able to ski fluently in all of them. He must be able to choose the best line and lead others confidently.

APPENDIX 5
Glossary

Alpine events: Generic term for the downhill ski competitions (giant slalom, slalom, and downhill).

Avalement: French term for 'swallowing' the variations in terrain during turns, by using the knees as springs.

BirdNesting: Off-*piste* skiing.

Chattering: Noise made by skis at speed as a result of vibration.

Christies: Family of turns originating from the Christiana (Oslo) region of Norway.

*Crud (*or *Crust) :* Nasty, crusty snow.

Draguer: Literally, to dredge. Colloquially, to go looking for an *après-ski* pick up. Beware of pronunciation—soften the 'g' and it becomes *dragée*, a sugared almond or laxative pill.

Fall line: The most direct line down the slope. Roll a ball and it will take the fall line.

FIS: The International Ski Federation (the acronym is from the French).

Föhn: Warm alpine wind that can rapidly change snow conditions.

GLM: Graduated Length Method of ski tuition.

Gunbarrel: Narrow trail with sloping sides like a giant gutter.

Harsch: Heavy snow with frozen surface.

Langlauf: German word, and the most widely used term for cross-country skiing.

Moguls: A pattern of 'mole-hills' in the snow, caused by skiers persistently turning at the same points.

Nordic events: The cross-country events in ski competitions.

Piste: A ski run.

Ratrac: Machine for packing the snow on runs.

Rotation: Assisting turns by rotating the upper body.

Ruade: Kicking out of heels on a down unweighted turn.

Ski de fond: French for cross-country skiing.

Ski évolutif: Ski tuition which uses gradually lengthening skis as the pupil improves. See GLM.

186

Schuss: Run straight down the fall line.

Telemark turn: An elegant curtsy-style turn rarely seen today.

Wedeln: A series of flowing linked turns. Once regarded as ski perfection and still the most elegant ski form. Best done without perceptible edging.

Wax: Wax is applied to the base surface of skis to improve their performance.

Vorlage: Once-popular ski posture involving extreme forward leaning from the ankles.

BIBLIOGRAPHY

Aikman, Alison and Parker, John, *Avis Guide to Skiing in Europe* (FMP Publications, London, 1974)

Bass, Howard, *Winter Sports* (Stanley Paul, London, 1966)

Beattie, Bob, *My Ten Secrets of Skiing* (Arthur Barker, London, 1968)

Brady, M. Michael, *Nordic Skiing* (Dreyers Forlag, Oslo, 1971)

De Linde, C. A., *Your Guide to Skiing Resorts* (Alvin Redman, London, 1965)

Evans, Harold; Jackman, Brian; Ottaway, Mark—Sunday Times, *We Learned to Ski* (Collins, London, 1974)

Heller, Mark, *All About Skiing* (Hamlyn, London, 1969)

Heller, Mark, *Leisure Guide: Skiing* (Macmillan, London, 1974)

Heller, Mark, *Ski* (Faber & Faber, London, 1969)

Heller, Mark, *Ski Guide—Austria* (Quartet, London, 1973)

Kramer, Franz, *Ski the New Way* (Bailey Bros and Swinfen, Folkestone, 1970)

Reilly, A. M., *Skiing: A Beginner's Guide* (Lutterworth Press, London, 1970)

Riddell, James and Jeannette, *Ski Holidays in the Alps* (Penguin, London, 1961)

Ross, David (ed.), *The Skier's Holiday Guide* (Ski Specialists, London, annually)

Shedden, John, *Ski Teaching* (John Jones Cardiff, Cardiff, 1972)

Ski Magazine's Expert Tips for Better Skiing (Harper and Row, New York, 1972)

Wiedmann, Otti, *The Skier's Pocket Book* (Pinguin-Verlag, Innsbruck, 1973)

INDEX